Who the Hell is Jean-Jacques Rousseau?

Who the Hell is Jean-Jacques Rousseau?

And what are his theories all about?

Cressida Tweed

BOWDEN
&BRAZIL

First published in Great Britain in 2020 by
Bowden & Brazil Ltd
Felixstowe, Suffolk, UK.

ISBN 978-1-9999492-9-7

To find out more about other books and authors in this series,
visit www.whothehellis.co.uk

Contents

Introduction

Jean-Jacques Rousseau is one of the most influential political philosophers of the 18th century. However, in his lifetime he was equally revered as despised, and this is still very much the case today. While some argue he set the foundations for a fairer society based on justice and equality, others see him as the godfather of totalitarianism. Few can deny, however, that he was an original and revolutionary thinker and writer, who turned our ideas of humankind, education, and what makes a 'good' society upside down. Rousseau himself lived through turbulent times and lived a tumultuous life. He craved isolation and solitude, finding solace and peace in nature, yet he lived in busy cities – Paris, Turin, Geneva – in the public eye. Not only was he a famous thinker but he lived as a real celebrity. He philosophized on the morals of love yet was far from exemplary in his own love and family life.

Rousseau's influence on contemporary political thought was huge. He argued that individuals must sacrifice their self-interest for the common good, and that a good society is one which is built on the will of its people – all its people – and not just that of the rich, the powerful, or the intelligentsia. These ideas would go on to influence the key players of the French Revolution who overtook the monarchy and instituted a French republic; and his notion of liberty and the idea that freedom is only possible if all are equal was a precursor to Marxism.

When it came to education, Rousseau's theories are considered to be the foundation of modern pedagogy. He argued that the purpose of education should not be to brainwash children into conventional and socially acceptable thought, but that instead, we should let children be free thinkers in order to develop fully. His love for the natural world and his writing on love and virtue made him one of the first romantics.

Rousseau had plenty of personal flaws, which made him the source of endless jibes and criticisms from fellow thinkers. His treatise on education and his philosophy of moral goodness, virtue and compassion seems at odds with his private choices: he had many mistresses while living with his common-law wife, Thérèse Levasseur, who bore him five children – all of whom were abandoned as babies to an orphanage.

Despite all this, however, most of which he recognizes in his autobiography *The Confessions* (1782), Rousseau is one of the most consistent and principled thinkers of his century. He stood by his beliefs despite his criticism of religion and monarchy leading to his books being burned, his life threatened and eventual life in exile which made him fearful and paranoid.

His faith in the innate, inherent goodness of mankind; his recognition that a society built on private interest feeds inequality and cannot truly flourish; his idea that the aim of society is a common good; that the people as a whole must be sovereign and have political authority, can only resonate with us and the problems we face today in the 21st century.

Who the Hell is Jean-Jacques Rousseau? will look at the key events of Rousseau's life and his influences along the way. We will look at why he deserves his status as a key thinker of the modern age, considering the three key ideas in Rousseau's philosophical thought: his understanding of humankind in the state of nature and the reason for inequality; his social contract (what we could call his ideal society); and his theory on education. All arguments are connected and stem from Rousseau's faith in human beings and his optimism in the possibility of improving the human condition.

1. Rousseau's Life Story

Jean-Jacques Rousseau was born in Geneva, Switzerland, on 28 June 1712. His father, Isaac Rousseau (1672–1747), was a modest watchmaker who was well-educated for an artisan by the standards of the day, and passionate about music. Jean-Jacques' mother, Suzanne Bernard (1672–1712), beautiful, musical and spirited, came from an upper-class family, having been raised by her uncle, a Calvinist preacher. Isaac and Suzanne had known each other and been inseparable since they were children and, despite the Bernards' disapproval of the match, the couple were married and began their life together.

Thanks to Suzanne's dowry, the couple were able to live comfortably in the fashionable part of Geneva until, following a general economic slump, the Rousseaus found themselves in financial difficulty. Only three months after their first child, François, was born, and perhaps also partly due to the newly arrived presence of his disapproving mother-in-law, Isaac left for Constantinople to take up a position as watchmaker to the Sultan (or so he claimed, although there is no evidence to support this). He was away for a full six years, returning home a year after Suzanne's mother had died and Suzanne had inherited 10,000 florins.

A Motherless Child

Nine months after Isaac's return, Jean-Jacques was born. Tragically, only a few days after giving birth, Suzanne died from puerperal fever at the age of just 39. In total, Isaac had spent only two years of married life with his wife, but now alone, his youngest sister, also called Suzanne, moved in to help with the children. Essentially she acted as a mother for the young Jean-Jacques and he grew close to his aunt, calling her 'Suzon'.

At the time of Jean-Jacques' birth, Geneva was a fairly large city, made up mostly of craftspeople and artisans. It was at that time a Protestant autonomous city surrounded by Catholic countries, and was ruled by a small social elite composed of rich families. Isaac Rousseau was deeply critical of this powerful oligarchy, and the young Jean-Jacques would also grow up with a strong belief in the sovereignty of the people, having seen how the Genevan oligarchy were betraying the idea of democracy. These ideas would later find themselves in *The Social Contract* (1762)

Originally from France, Isaac's family made their way to Geneva to escape political persecution. Isaac was well read and involved in the political circle and, as a consequence, the first 10 years of the young Rousseau's life were spent overhearing political debates and revolutionary ideals. His father read novels to him, as well as the classics of Ancient Greek and Roman literature, with Jean-Jacques learning Plutarch by heart. He treated his son as an equal, allowing him to develop in his own way and they shared a rather eccentric love of Suzanne's romantic novels and would take turns reading them out loud to one another. According to Rousseau, all this precocious reading 'gave me bizarre and romantic notions of human life, which experience and reflection have never been able to cure me of' (quoted in Damrosch, 2007). All in all, Isaac's influence on Jean-Jacques' early childhood and his learning was profound. Although he never received a formal education, his copious appetite for literature allowed him to develop all the necessary skills in order to become a master of French prose.

However, Isaac could also be selfish, argumentative and wholly unreliable, thinking nothing of abandoning his family. When Rousseau was five and his brother 12, Isaac sold Suzanne's house for a fairly large amount of money. The proceeds were meant to be held in trust for both boys until they were 25 years old, with Isaac living off the interest. However, over time, Rousseau's father succeeded in getting his hands on most of the money. When Rousseau was 10 years old, his father became embroiled in a fight with a French captain and rather than face prison, chose to leave Geneva forever, taking his sister Suzon with him. Abandoned by both their father and their mother-figure, care of the two boys was given over to their mother's family – the Bernards. Jean-Jacques made the occasional visit to his father in Nyon, where he had settled, but Isaac showed little interest. Suzon got married and seems to have had very little to do with her nephews from that time on.

Happiness in Bossey

After their father's abrupt departure from Geneva, the Bernards found an apprenticeship for François while sending Jean-Jacques and his cousin, Abraham, to live with the pastor Lambercier and his sister Gabrielle in Bossey – a village just outside the city walls. The two cousins became inseparable, depending on one another for emotional security. The pastor had been appointed to teach the boys Latin and educate them generally, including religious instruction, although his efforts were far from stringent.

The two years Rousseau spent in Bossey were some of the happiest of his life. He discovered a passion for the natural world that would never leave him and his days were filled with lessons, walks, games in nature and attempts at planting trees. His religious beliefs were fundamentally Calvinist, which gave great importance to psalms and which Jean-Jacques adored, as he had a great love for music. However, it was here that Rousseau encountered his first injustice: accused of breaking a comb, his uncle Gabriel was written to and sent for, and Rousseau was beaten for it. He always protested his innocence but quickly learned that you can appear to be guilty even when you are innocent. The incident left him feeling indignant and betrayed by adults who did not believe him. He recounted this moment in his *Confessions* (1782) some 50 years later and felt that this was the moment he lost his purity and innocence as a child. He writes:

> *'Imagine a character, timid and docile in ordinary circumstances, but ardent, proud and indomitable when roused; a child who has always been governed by the voice of reason, always treated with tenderness, equity, indulgence; who has no notion, even of injustice, and who for the first time experiences a terrible example of it at the hands of precisely those people whom he loves and respects the most. What havoc in his ideas? What confusion in his feelings? What an upheaval in his little heart, in his brain, in his whole moral and intellectual being!'* (Rousseau, 1782)

This indignation at injustice is something that would form the basis of Rousseau's philosophy; from childhood he saw both the injustice of society and how it corrupts humankind. He argued throughout his writing career that primitive humans, living in a state of nature, become depraved once they become social animals, forming societies, and that 'society' as we know it is inherently unjust.

At the age of 13, Rousseau was sent back to Geneva to start work as an apprentice; first to the city notary at the *hôtel de ville*, which he hated, then with an engraver called Abel Ducommun. At first Rousseau enjoyed the work – he was good at drawing and liked using the tools – but it wasn't to last. Ducommun was a brute and a bully and Rousseau was badly treated and missed the challenges of more intellectual surroundings. Perhaps in retaliation, he resorted to petty theft, for which he was found out. Reflecting on this time in his *Confessions*, he felt once again corrupted by the other people around him. He couldn't see a future for himself in Geneva as a craftsman and dreamt of a better life. One thing the apprenticeship had taught him was that he abhorred being made to work for others. He could settle to a task with exactitude and concentration, but only if it was self-appointed.

From Annecy to Turin and Back

By the age of 16, Rousseau had had enough. Returning from a walk one Sunday, he missed the curfew and found the doors to the city locked (like many European cities, Geneva was then surrounded by fortifications). For Rousseau, this was a sign for him to leave and after two days of wandering he found refuge in the house of a Catholic priest in Confignon, a few miles from Geneva. The priest recommended that he travel to Annecy, where there was a kind Catholic lady who might be willing to take him under her protection. This next encounter would be the most important one in his life.

Françoise-Louise-Eléonore de la Tour, Baroness de Warens (1699–1762) was a Catholic convert who had left her husband and home near Lausanne and lived under the protection of the King of Sardinia, who also ruled over the Savoie province at that time. The King gave her an allowance in return for helping and guiding people who had converted from Protestantism to Catholicism. This meeting was life-changing for Rousseau, and over the next three days he became completely smitten with the 29-year-old woman. Madame de Warens was young, beautiful and charismatic. Recalling the first time they met in his *Confessions*, Rousseau remarks:

> *'This was the period of my life that decided my character.*
> *I cannot bring myself to pass over it lightly [...]*
> *Nothing escaped the rapid glance of the young proselyte;*
> *for I became hers on the spot, convinced that a religion*
> *preached by such missionaries could lead only to paradise.'*
> (Rousseau, 1782)

Mme de Warens sent Rousseau to Turin, which was then the capital of the Savoie province, to complete his Catholic conversion. Having run out of money he found work as a footman for a dying Comtesse, for whom he dictated letters. It was here that an incident occurred which would always stay with him and which triggered one of his many insights. After the Comtesse's death, Rousseau spotted a silver ribbon among her things, which he pocketed. However, unfortunately for him, there was a comprehensive inventory and the ribbon was missed and found in his room. He blamed a young sweet-natured cook, Marion, who denied it vehemently. Rousseau recounts in his *Confessions*, 'the Count de la Roque, in sending us both away, contented himself with saying, "The conscience of the guilty would revenge the innocent." His prediction was true, and is being daily verified'. Looking back on the incident, he reflects that it was the fear of being publicly shamed and called a thief and a liar to his face that induced him to lie, and that it would be the last time he would ever be dishonest. Indeed, as Damrosch writes in his biography, 'The heart of Rousseau's later thinking lies in this little incident, which no other writer of the time would have been likely to relate. To liberate the authentic self from socially induced hypocrisy and deception would become his mission.' (2007)

It was also in Turin that Rousseau met the priest Jean-Claude Gaime, who would be the template for the Savoyard vicar in Rousseau's *Émile* (1762). Gaime made a deep impression on the insecure youngster, helping him to regain some self-confidence and coaxing him to make something of his life. Rousseau took up another position of footman, this time to the Comte de Gouvon, where he made quite an impression with his knowledge of Latin. He spent a lot of his spare time walking in the countryside, sometimes with Gaime, but mostly alone. Rousseau always connected his love of nature with religious emotion – a unique sentiment in his day, but one that would become widespread with the onset of Romanticism.

Rousseau's life-long dislike of working under other people's orders soon showed itself again, this time taking the form of acting irresponsibly with another young member of the household staff, and generally being 'delinquent' (Damrosch, 2007). A dismissal from the Comte inevitably occurred and Rousseau took to the road once again, heading back to Mme de Warens.

Happiness in Chambéry and Les Charmettes

Mme de Warens welcomed Rousseau back and an intense and complex relationship began. Before long he began calling her *Maman* (mother), while she referred to him as *mon petit* (my little one). She had no children, and Rousseau became emotionally reliant on her during his time in Chambéry. They shared the lack of a mother – Françoise de la Tour (later de Warens) had lost her mother at the age of one, and the aunt who then cared for her (much as Suzon had cared for Rousseau) died when Françoise was just 10 years old. She never found a stable home again during her childhood, and had sought comfort in music, as Rousseau had also done. On many occasions de Warens sent him away, with the intention of helping him to find a profession that matched his talents. First he went to a seminary to study for the priesthood, later writing: 'I went to the seminary as I would have gone to be tortured. What a gloomy house a seminary is, especially for someone who is leaving the house of a charming woman!' (Damrosch, 2007) After a few months, he transferred to the tutelage of the music master of the cathedral to take music instruction, but as he explains in his *Confessions*:

> *'...the fear of not learning prevents my being attentive,*
> *and a dread of wearying those who teach, makes me*

feign to understand them; thus they proceed faster than
I can comprehend, and the conclusion is I learn nothing.
My understanding must take its own time and cannot
submit to that of another.' (Rousseau, 1782)

Rousseau spent a year travelling: from Fribourg to Lausanne and Neuchâtel, briefly in Paris, then to Lyon. He had worked at his music along the way and by this time become a reasonably competent musician. But more importantly, these long journeys – which he mostly did on foot – gave him the opportunity to have many a 'reverie' as he called it. Many of these thoughts, which came to him while walking, would form the basis for some of his most important ideas later on. His many encounters, too, with people from all walks of life, fashioned his political opinions, 'sowing seeds of that inextinguishable hatred which has grown in my heart against the vexations these unhappy people suffer, and against their oppressors' (Rousseau, 1782). Having experienced his own fair share of injustice, Rousseau was beginning to see that injustice in society was fundamental to the way it functioned.

The final leg of his journey took him to Chambéry, now the home of his beloved *Maman*. He took up a job at the land registry, in which he lasted eight months, then began to pursue his passion for music instead, submerging himself in complicated works of music theory by the composer Jean-Philippe Rameau. And so began a time of contentment. Mme de Warens introduced him to the local aristocracy and taught him social conventions; he learnt fencing, studied botany and played chess. He also read voraciously: philosophy, the classics, music, astronomy, history, algebra, anything he could get his hands on.

Fig. 1 "Les Charmettes" where Rousseau stayed with Mme de Warens.

His role as a music teacher began to pick up pace and, being easily seduced by charming young people, Rousseau found himself living a life of pleasant flirtation. His dalliances never went any further however, as his Calvinist upbringing and pious nature had instilled in him anxieties about sex. Mme de Warens would be the first woman he had sexual relations with yet, as he admitted in his *Confessions*, 'I felt I know not what invincible sadness which empoisoned my happiness, it seemed that I had committed an incest'. She had filled the role of mother, sister and friend for Rousseau, and he 'loved her too much to desire her'.

In 1735, after a bout of illness, Rousseau moved to a rural retreat with Mme de Warens. Just outside of Chambéry, Les Charmettes was a haven of peace and tranquillity. He would look back at his time spent there as one of true happiness, even though illness would continue to dog him. The doctor who was looking after him (and who was a disciple of Descartes) encouraged Rousseau to read, conversing with him on philosophy and science, and over the next two years, he devoured works by Voltaire, Descartes, Plato, Locke and Leibniz, to name but a few. He taught himself geometry, algebra and calculus, and even tried to teach himself astronomy. However, he was becoming a burden on Mme de Warens, who could no longer afford to support him. She found him a position as tutor for a wealthy family in Lyon and he was obliged to accept.

From Paris to Venice

Rousseau arrived in Lyon in 1739 and made many valuable connections there among the intelligentsia, at a time when the Enlightenment had just begun. One in particular – Étienne Bonnot de Condillac, a philosopher – would prove invaluable to Rousseau later on in Paris. Rousseau's work as a tutor was not particularly successful but it gave him the opportunity to theorize on the nature of learning itself, which would eventually take the form of his famous treatise on education, *Émile*. In a memorandum that he put together for his employer, he touched upon contemporary progressive theories, showing his understanding that children have to want to learn themselves, and that their different temperaments require different techniques. His memorandum also reveals a bluntly honest self-portrait of his perceived characteristics which would come to be seen as 'inseparable from Rousseau's greatness as a thinker and writer' (Damrosch, 2007). A year later, tiring of tutoring, Rousseau made one last trip back to Chambéry to see Mme de Warens, but their relationship had come to an end. Disappointed by her rejection of him, he understood that she had nonetheless given him more than anyone else had in his life: security, affection, time and money to educate himself, and above all, she had believed in him. By 1742, it was time for him to go to Paris.

Having struggled with musical scores all his life, Rousseau decided to create a simpler system of musical notation and present it to the Academy of Sciences in Paris. Alas, although his effort was commended, his method was not as original as he had thought: the Academy pointed out that his proposal indicated melody but not harmony. Running low on money, Rousseau took up first a tutoring job, then a secretarial job to the Dupins, a rich Parisian family. Through his Lyon connections, he found himself introduced into the famous Paris salons – gatherings hosted by notable women in wealthy houses. While this presented Rousseau with an opportunity to meet the right people, he was cripplingly shy in large groups, preferring to talk to one or two people at a time. In *Julie* (1761), we get an insight into his feelings at this time through his character Saint-Preux, who describes his experience of Paris and the salons as being wholly insincere: 'biting and satiric laughter is the sorry substitute for the gaiety that no longer exists [...] Woe to him who lays himself open to ridicule; its caustic imprint is ineradicable.'

In 1743, Rousseau was offered a job as secretary to the French ambassador, the Comte de Montaigu, in Venice. Although he disliked his employer and was disliked in return, this short episode in his life did much to booster his self-confidence and self-esteem. Due to Montaigu's ineptitude at his job, Rousseau found himself taking on more and more responsibility for the embassy, and discovered a capability that he (and everyone else) had been quite unaware that he possessed. Having learnt Italian in Turin when he was a boy, he was by now quite fluent at the language and was particularly taken with the spontaneity and beauty of Italian music, delighting in the fact that all the concerts and operas were affordable to everyone. The short period that he spent in Venice was clearly important to him as half of Book VII of his *Confessions* was devoted to this time. Hinting at how his ideas developed during this period, Rousseau remarks:

> *'I had an opportunity of remarking the defects of that government so much boasted of, conceived the first idea of them [...] I had perceived everything to be radically connected with politics, and that upon whatever principles these were founded, a people would never be more than that which the nature of the government made them [...] What is the nature of a government the most proper to form the most virtuous and enlightened, the wisest and best people, taking the last epithet in its most extensive meaning?'* (Rousseau, 1782)

Following a final confrontation with Montaigu, Rousseau returned to Paris in 1744, nursing a new grudge that those in inferior positions are always deemed to be in the wrong.

A Life-long Companion and a Secret

Returning to his old lodgings in rue des Cordiers, it was here that Rousseau met Thérèse Levasseur, a laundry girl who would become his life-long companion for the next 33 years. Rousseau's peers looked down on his choice of partner and he defended himself by saying that their relationship was one of convenience. Indeed he states in his *Confessions* that 'from the very moment that I saw her until today, I have never felt the least spark of love for her'. However it seems likely that she meant a good deal more to him than he liked to admit. In many parts of his autobiography, he sings her praises, describing her as having the heart 'of an angel' and going on to say 'our attachment increased with our intimacy, and we were more and more daily convinced how much we were made for each other.'

In 1746, Thérèse fell pregnant with the first of five children. All of the couple's babies were given immediately to a foundling home – the Hôpital des Enfants-Trouvés (Hospital of abandoned children). This part of Rousseau's history has shocked many; not only because Rousseau suffered abandonment in various forms himself as a child, but because he wrote *Émile*, a book on how to bring up children (see Chapter 5).

The only existing evidence of why Rousseau chose to give up his children are his own words in his *Confessions*:

> *'I made up my mind to take it, blithely and without the last scruple; indeed, the only one with which I had to contend came from Thérèse, whom I had the greatest difficulty in the world in persuading to adopt the only course of action that would preserve her honour. But when her mother, who feared, in addition, the burden of another child, came to my aid, she let herself be overruled. We chose a discreet and reliable midwife called Mlle Gouin, who lived at the far end of Saint-Eustache, to whom we felt we could entrust this task and, when her time came, Thérèse was taken by her mother to Mlle Gouin's house to be delivered. [...] The child was then deposited by the midwife at the bureau*

*for foundlings, according to the normal procedure. The
following year the same inconvenience presented itself,
the same expedient was adopted.'* (Rousseau, 1782)

While his words sound rather callous, Rousseau claims
reasons of poverty and honour – Thérèse was unmarried, the
children would have had no social status, Rousseau was poor and
was supporting not only Thérèse but also her mother and her
extended family. It seems he truly felt that the children's fate at an
orphanage would be better than a life spent with the Levasseurs,
who he found to be unscrupulous and dishonest. Certainly, it
was far from exceptional for unmarried mothers to abandon their
children at that time: around 5,000 children in Paris were left to
foundling homes during that period.

Whatever his reasons, he does express regrets. In Book IX of
his *Confessions*, he says:

> *'the decision I had come to with regards to my children,
> however well considered it had seemed to me to be, had
> left me with a heart that was not always easy. While
> pondering my treatise on education, I had come to feel I
> had neglected duties from which nothing could absolve
> me.'* (Rousseau, 1782)

But for many critics, it is not the abandonment itself that is
so shocking, but the fact that Rousseau felt creditable to write
Émile. For Monique Cottret, in her book *Jean-Jacques Rousseau
en son Temps* (2011), his remorse was the very reason that he did
write *Émile* and it is certainly evident in Rousseau's section on
'The New-Born Child':

'He who cannot fulfil the duties of a father has no right to be a father. Not poverty, nor severe labor, nor human respect can release him from the duty of supporting his children and of educating them himself. Readers, you may believe my words. I prophesy to any one who has natural feeling and neglects these sacred duties,—that he will long shed bitter tears over this fault, and that for those tears he will find no consolation.' (Rousseau, 1889)

The *Encyclopédie*

Rousseau spent the next few years trying to succeed as a musician, writing ballets, but with no success. Some thought his musical works merely a bid for recognition, but, as Damrosch points out in his biography, 'music meant far more to him than that. [...] Melody imitates emotion [...] for Rousseau even instrumental music had to sing' (2007).

While in Paris, Rousseau met the philosopher Denis Diderot, whose friendship would have a marked effect on his life. They were both sons of artisans so had not come from money. However, whereas Rousseau was shy and unconfident, Diderot was headstrong and sure of himself, with a habit of physically grabbing those he was conversing with to ensure their attention. He had arrived in Paris at 16 to study at the Sorbonne and been living a bohemian lifestyle as a philosopher and writer ever since, supporting himself through maths tutoring and various publishing jobs.

Rousseau was supporting himself through secretarial and research work for the Dupins, both of whom were occupied with writing projects. Probably his longest term of employment, this lasted from

1746 to 1751. In the meantime, he began to spend a lot of time with Diderot and Condillac (whom he'd met in Lyon). Along with another friend, Jean le Rond d'Alembert – another great thinker – they would all meet regularly for dinners where they would engage in lively intellectual discussions. This would prove an indispensable influence on Rousseau's development as a thinker and writer (see Chapter 2).

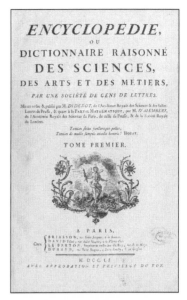

Fig. 2 Diderot's *Encyclopedia.*

Of the many projects that they embarked on together, the *Encyclopedic Dictionary of the Arts and Sciences* – the *Encyclopedia* – was the most extraordinary. The brainchild of Diderot, this vast project set out to combine all human knowledge in a way that was democratic and accessible. Published in 1751, it became the heart of the Enlightenment movement, questioning established morality, religion and dogmatism. It soon became a weapon against the establishment itself, and (unsurprisingly) was quickly denounced by both the Church and the King of France. The *Encyclopedia* would eventually include 72,000 articles, written between 1751 and 1772, with almost 400 articles written by Rousseau on politics and music.

The Illumination of Vincennes

In 1749, following a crackdown on criticisms against the government, Diderot was arrested and imprisoned in Vincennes for three months. His friends visited him often; Rousseau made the trek of several miles every few days. It was on one such occasion that he received what he calls an illumination. While walking, he was reading the *Mercure de France* journal, which he subscribed to, and noticed a competition put forward by the Academy of Dijon for an essay. The question was 'Has the restoration of the sciences and arts contributed to the purification of morals?'. He started to think deeply about the purpose of arts and science within society and about their effect on human nature and the human condition. He argued, paradoxically, that civilization has brought about both advancement and destruction; the downfalls being a direct consequence of the virtues. He writes,

> *'Suspicions, offences, fears, coldness, reserve, hatred, and betrayal will always be hiding under this uniform and perfidious veil of politeness, under that urbanity which is so praised and which we owe to our century's enlightenment.'* (Rousseau, 1750)

He didn't find it easy to sit and write, preferring instead to compose and re-compose paragraphs in his head while walking or lying in bed, before committing them to paper. But once he did finally write down his ideas they 'had an oracular power that no other writer of his time even aspired to' (Damrosch, 2007). To his great surprise, he won the competition and – thanks to his friend Guillaume Raynal, editor of the *Mercure de France*, who gave it ample coverage – Rousseau instantly became famous. The response to his discourse was huge – 75 reviews and critiques – and Rousseau certainly proved himself to be up to the job of responding to his critics respectfully and intelligently.

His fame at last began to open doors and, with renewed belief in himself, he threw himself into his music, writing an opera in a few weeks. *Le Devin du Village*, or *The Village Soothsayer*, was played at the royal court at Fontainebleau to huge acclaim. King Louis XV, very much taken with the music, asked to meet Rousseau which strongly implied a pension would be offered. However, much to everyone's surprise, he ignored the invitation and returned to Paris the very next day. Everyone tried to reason with him, confounded by his behaviour, but the explanation that he gave was his ongoing urinary problem that had dogged him for many years and which caused him to need to urinate constantly. On social occasions this gave him much embarrassment which would have added to his already deep-rooted discomfort and fear in large – and especially aristocratic – social situations.

While this may have been true, more importantly Rousseau was determined to remain independent and not tied to the royal court, since he would have been obliged to follow what was socially and politically acceptable. He had already made up his mind to live by the principles set out in his *Discourse*, which he had come to see didn't follow the philosophy of the encyclopedists, resulting in him distancing himself from Diderot and the others. Not only did he abhor their active atheism, but also their focus on science and reason: technical progress was entirely contrary to his *Discourse on the Sciences and Arts*.

Rousseau's rejection of social and political norms also extended itself to the music establishment. He made it known that to be accomplished in music one did not have to be a trained expert, but simply understand music from the heart. He then took this further by criticizing French music, comparing it to (in his opinion) superior Italian music. Needless to say, he caused some offence and soon became the *bête noire* of the music world.

The *Second Discourse*

In 1754, Rousseau once again entered an essay competition from the Academy of Dijon on the following question: 'What is the origin of inequality among men, and is it authorized by natural law?' Ignoring the length requirement and writing an essay of 100 pages, his *Second Discourse*, as it became known, was very much the starting point of his philosophical system. Although it didn't win and was generally not as well received as the first one, it did reveal his strength as a writer. It was published the following year as *Discourse on the Origin and Foundations of Inequality among Men* and it showed just how far his thinking had developed (see Chapter 3).

However, by now his writing was beginning to raise concern: he was undermining the legitimacy of the rich and the powerful with his treatises on how humanity was alienated and suffering. Key thinkers of that time accused Rousseau of being envious and resentful. Voltaire in particular was very critical and wrote a scathing reply to the *Discourse*, saying:

> 'I have received your new book against the human race, and thank you for it. [...] No one has ever employed so much intellect to persuade men to be beasts. In reading your work one is seized with a desire to walk on all fours. However, as I have lost that habit for more than sixty years, I feel, unfortunately, that it is impossible for me to resume it.' (Letter from Voltaire to Rousseau, 30 August 1755)

This response triggered a lifelong enmity between the two men, who never met and communicated only through letters. Voltaire would never understand Rousseau's disgust of the price that had to be paid by many for advancements that benefitted only a few. He would never see that Rousseau's life experience had given him the authority to speak on inequality, and that he wore it as a badge of honour. For many, Rousseau's treatise was full of paradoxes, but it is this that made it so original. As Damrosch sums up:

> *'It was common to criticize specific inequities in society and to appeal for reform, but original to hold that inequality is both unacceptable and inevitable. It was common to acknowledge that labor could be harsh, but original to define it as a fundamental betrayal of our essential nature. It was common to say that we learn to see ourselves as others see us and become integrated with society, but original to describe that process as a betrayal of our true selves.'* (Damrosch, 2007)

Madame d'Epinay

Rousseau's *Discourse* was noticed by Mme d'Epinay, an aristocrat and a writer on education and women's rights. Wishing to broaden her intellectual milieu, she offered Rousseau a cottage near her country house in Montmorency, just outside Paris. Having been recently renovated, The Hermitage was too irresistible for Rousseau to turn down and, though refusing the pension of 1,000 livres she offered him, he let himself be persuaded to move in with Thérèse and her mother. There he led a simple life, enjoying

Fig. 3 Portrait of Jean-Jacques Rousseau painted by Maurice Quentin de La Tour in 1753.

the tranquillity and distance from the 'civilization' of Paris.

Things were, however, to turn sour. His relationship with Mme d'Epinay was somewhat temperamental, due to Rousseau's inability to accept her patronage, seeing her demands on his attention as the power play of a superior class. Worse, when her sister-in-law, Sophie d'Houdetot, arrived, Rousseau fell head over heels in love. While their relationship lasted no more than a month, it drove a wedge between Rousseau, Mme d'Epinay, and eventually Sophie d'Houdetot, too. It was at this point that Rousseau began to believe that there was a plot against him – suspicions of which had begun in Paris with his colleagues on the *Encyclopedia* – and which instigated a series of letters from Rousseau that did little to ingratiate him to his friends and acquaintances.

Rousseau's epistolary novel, *Julie* or *La Nouvelle Heloise*, is thought to have been inspired by Sophie d'Houdetot. Published in 1761, it became a bestseller and was reprinted 12 times between 1761 and 1800, a feat unheard of at the time. Librarians even offered to rent it for a small sum for those who could not afford to buy a copy. Six months after his novel went to press, Rousseau was sought out by the Duc de Luxembourg, who had been unsuccessfully trying to make Rousseau's acquaintance for a while. He would become Rousseau's most loyal supporter, as well as a cherished friend, and his patronage was offered with no expectations. It was on these terms that Rousseau moved with Thérèse into a villa on the Luxembourg's estate.

A Life in Exile

Estranged from his old friends and encouraged by his new, Rousseau threw himself into his writing, working on what would become two of his most acclaimed works – *The Social Contract* (see Chapter 4) and *Émile* (see Chapter 5), both of which were published in 1762. Both texts would be considered controversial by the Parisian intelligentsia, as well as the Church and the monarchy, and were subsequently banned in France. The French parliament made it known that Rousseau was to be arrested and so, with the help of the Luxembourgs, he left France and began his journey in exile.

Over the next eight years, Rousseau would live in many different places but each time his reputation would catch up with him and he would be forced to leave. Heading first to Switzerland, he was forbidden to stay by the authorities, but finding a supporter in George Keith – the governor of the Swiss canton of Neuchâtel – he found refuge for two years in Môtiers, before local ministers became aware of the nature of his works and he was again forced to leave. After an all-too-brief stay on L'île St-Pierre, in the middle of the Lac de Bienne, Rousseau headed for England.

It was now 1766. The Scottish philosopher David Hume was working at the British Embassy in Paris as *chargé d'affaires* (a type of ambassador). Offering to settle Rousseau in England, they travelled together to London where Hume took him to the theatre and introduced him into society. However, it didn't take long before Hume began to tire of his guest, finding him highly strung and absurdly eccentric. Rousseau's paranoia gradually got worse and he accused Hume of working against him and conniving with his enemies, especially the thinkers of the *Encyclopedia*. In fact the campaign against him was real, but did not stem from Hume, whose covert actions were simply to help Rousseau financially without wanting to appear condescending to him. Unfortunately the Encyclopedists encouraged Hume to publicly defend himself against Rousseau's accusations and, fearful for his reputation, Hume acquiesced. Partly self-inflicted but by no means entirely, Rousseau found himself a public figure vilified as a madman.

The Final Years

Returning to France in 1767, Rousseau spent the next three years in abject misery. He found it impossible to trust anyone and lived in a constant state of dread, both from the French authorities who still had a warrant out for his arrest, and from his own paranoid obsession that everyone was against him. It seems that believing this had become part of who he was. As Damrosch puts it:

> *'It explained his feeling of undeserved and perpetual isolation, and it gave him a way to project his gnawing sense of guilt onto agents outside himself, with a Lear-like sense of loss, grief, and undeserved suffering.'* (Damrosch, 2007)

During this time he finally married Thérèse and, living under a false name with his health failing him, he spent his time writing

Fig. 4 The tomb of Jean-Jacques Rousseau in the Panthéon in Paris, France.

his *Confessions*. Finally returning to Paris to face his fears, he discovered that the government were prepared to leave him alone as long as he kept quiet. And so, in his final years, he lived in seclusion, continuing his work copying music and following his passion for botany. Although he made new acquaintances, he mostly kept to himself. Upon finishing the *Confessions*, true to his word he did not publish it, so as not to embarrass those still living, but instead embarked on private readings to those he deemed influential. By 1778, his health and consequently, income, were rapidly declining. Invited by one of his admirers, the Marquis de Girardin, to come and live at his château in Ermenonville, just north of Paris, Rousseau and Thérèse made their final move. Rousseau spent the last of his days here, in tranquillity. On 2 July 1778, he complained to Thérèse of a splitting headache, chest pains and tingling feet before collapsing. He died just four days after his 66th birthday.

Jean-Jacques Rousseau 's Timeline

Rousseau	World Events

1712 Jean-Jacques Rousseau is born in Geneva; Suzanne Bernard, his mother, dies ten days later.

1715 King Louis XIV dies.

1722 Leaves Geneva to live in Bossey with his cousin.

1723 Louis XV becomes new King of France.

1725 Returns to Geneva to start work as an apprentice.

1728 Meets Mme de Warens and converts to Catholicism; travels to Turin.

1729 Moves in with Mme de Warens in Annecy.

1731 Settles in Chambery with Mme de Warens.

1735 Moves to Les Charmettes with Mme de Warens.

1740 British parliament grant British nationality to Huguenots and Jews in colonies.

1742 Leaves for Paris to present a system of musical notation to the Académie des sciences, which is rejected.

1742 Denmark and France sign a friendship treaty; French forces defeat Austrians in Battle of Sahay.

1743 Becomes secretary to the French ambassador in Venice.

1744 Returns to Paris and befriends Diderot.

1745 Meets Thérèse Levasseur.

1746 Becomes secretary to Mme Dupin.

1749 *First Discourse* wins the Académie de Dijon essay prize.

1749 Diderot imprisoned in the Chateau de Vincennes.

1752 Writes a pastoral opera *Le devin du village*	**1751** First articles of the *Encyclopedia* are published.
1754 Returns to Geneva, famous and celebrated; converts back to Protestantism.	
1755 *Second Discourse* is published.	
	1756 Seven Years' War begins, involving Western European countries and caused by dispute over land in the American Colonies.
1758 Lives in Montmorency and writes his letter to d'Alembert	
1761 *Julie* is published, becoming a best seller.	
1762 *The Social Contract* and *Émile* are published; both texts are banned in Paris and Geneva; arrest warrant issued in Paris; Rousseau flees to Switzerland.	**1763** End of Seven Years' War; France loses significant land in its American colonies.
1765 House in Motiers is stoned; Rousseau finds refuge in the L'Île St-Pierre but is soon expelled.	
1766 Starts writing *Les Rêveries*	**1766** Adam Smith publishes *The Wealth of Nations*.
	1778 France signs alliance with American rebel force and recognizes the United States of America as a sovereign nation; France's king, Louis XVI, declares war on Britain.
1778 Moves to Ermenonville and suffers a brain hemorrhage; dies aged 66	
1782 First part of *Confessions* is published	**1779** French Revolution begins.
1789 Second part of *Confessions* is published	
1794 Rousseau's remains moved to the Panthéon in Paris.	**1793** Louis XVI is executed by guillotine; Reign of Terror begins in France.

2. Influences on Rousseau's Thinking

Rousseau's influences were wide-ranging and encompassed people he met throughout his life as well as intellectuals that he interacted with or whose works he read along the way. An autodidact with no formal education, Rousseau was largely responsible for his own breadth of knowledge and immersed himself in the works of all the great thinkers.

His time as a tutor in Lyon and Paris, and his meeting with intellectuals, particularly Diderot and Condillac, shaped his understanding of human knowledge and the human condition, as well as his view of education. His work as a research assistant for a rich Parisian family led to him reading a vast amount of political and legal theory and formed the academic grounding of his theory of a just state. And finally, the philosophers of the Enlightenment and the Parisian intelligentsia allowed him to develop a truly original system of thought, a system considered dangerous by established political and religious powers and which made him the enemy of the intellectual circles who initially applauded him.

Republicanism and the Virtues of the Citizen

The influence of Rousseau's father cannot be underestimated, even though a significant part of Rousseau's childhood was spent away from him. As well as reading the works of Plutarch, Plato and Aristotle with the young Rousseau, Isaac also introduced his son to the world of politics. He was proud to be a master watchmaker and, educated and politically engaged, he was equally proud to be an active citizen in the small Genevan republic, with a keen sense of his rights and obligations. There is little doubt that Isaac instilled in Rousseau a love for his city but also shared with him an awareness of the problems and threats facing the Republic.

In the 18th century, Geneva was a city state similar to Venice or Florence, and its main trade was craftsmanship. It had been a Protestant stronghold from the time of the Reformation in the 16th century, welcoming Protestant refugees from France since 1523. John Calvin (1509–1564) was a French theologian and pastor who was the principal figure of the Protestant Reformation in Geneva and very much its spiritual leader. In 1536, Genevans took a public oath of allegiance to Protestantism and declared the city a republic, whereby the country was considered to be the concern of all members of the republic, rather than just the rulers. It was not dissimilar to a Classical city state and under the influence of Calvin, soon became the equivalent of Rome for the Protestant Church. As a republic, in principle, everyone had equal rights; in practice however, it played out that some had more rights than others. The reason for this was that Geneva was ruled by two councils: the Grand Conseil (General Council) was the council of all its citizens, while the Petit Conseil (Small Council) was made up of oligarchs and had the lion's share of power. This led to divisions in the city; the leading families who ruled the Petit Conseil had executive power and used their position to raise taxes that would cripple the middle classes. Being very pro-France, they showed little commitment to preserving the independence of the small republic, neither did they support Calvinism. The middle classes, largely craftspeople, were far more pious and devoted to republicanism. Over the next 20 years there was much unrest between the two factions and in the 1750s, a watchmaker called Jacques Francois Deluc formed a populist group of republicans calling themselves the *Répresentants* (the remonstrators) and led a campaign of resistance against the Oligarchy in order to gain fairer representation. Isaac Rousseau was very much a part of this resistance and the young Rousseau must have been greatly influenced by his father's politics, as will become evident in later chapters.

A Love/Hate Relationship

Although he left Geneva at the age of 16, Rousseau returned periodically over the years, his relationship with the city being a complex one. Throughout his life he saw himself as a Genevan citizen and patriot, yet he was quite often critical of Genevan institutions and its governance. Throughout his writings we see how his political thought, his defence of republicanism and democracy, and his religious puritanism are rooted in his Genevan origins, yet he saw clearly how these political ideals didn't necessary play out in practice.

In 1754, Deluc (who, along with his sons, would become strong defenders and supporters of Rousseau) wrote to him extolling the dedication he made to the city of Geneva and its citizens in his *Second Discourse*. Rousseau writes:

> *'My dear fellow-citizens, or rather my brothers, since the ties of blood, as well as the laws, unite almost all of us,*

it gives me pleasure that I cannot think of you, without
thinking, at the same time, of all the blessings you enjoy,
and of which none of you, perhaps, more deeply feels the
value than I who have lost them. The more I reflect on
your civil and political condition, the less can I conceive
that the nature of human affairs could admit of a better.'
(Rousseau, 1755)

Seemingly full of praise for the Genevan government, his intention was in fact quite the opposite. Helena Rosenblatt, who wrote extensively on Rousseau and Geneva, argues the following:

'Through ostensible flattery, Rousseau delivered an
ingenious criticism of the values of Geneva's patrician
magistrates as well as a strong warning about the
direction in which they were taking the republic.'
(Rosenblatt, 2006)

Although his dedication represented (to a degree) the ideal democratic institution – a republic with a deep political commitment of its citizens – Rousseau indirectly denounced the inequalities present in Geneva itself. He was very critical of the Genevan constitution, regarding its political system as tyrannical with the power held by a few and benefitting only a few rather than everyone. In practice, Geneva had become an aristocratic, oligarchic republic. The idea of a good state, which he would go on to develop in *The Social Contract*, was very much inspired by some of the republican ideals of Geneva – not as it stood in his time, but rather as it was when it was instituted as a Republic in the 16th century, when there were less political divisions and a more united community of spirits. It was Geneva's Grand Conseil that he had in mind when conceiving of a General Will, whereby he envisaged the sovereign as representing the people as a whole, with whoever ruled acting merely as a civil servant who carried out the will of the people. We will look at his argument in more detail in Chapter 4.

Calvinist Values

Rousseau's love for Geneva wasn't just love for its democratic potential and ideas, however, but also a love for its Calvinist values. We see this in his dispute with writer and philosopher Jean le Rond d'Alembert, whom he befriended in Paris while editing the *Encyclopedia*. In October 1757, d'Alembert wrote an article on Geneva for the *Encyclopedia*, denouncing Genevan puritanism and Calvinism, and arguing for the implementation of theatres in the city in order to develop free thinking and art.

In his *Letter to Alembert on the Theatre* (1758), Rousseau argued against the opening of theatres in Geneva, stating that such Parisian libertine pastimes would lead to its downfall:

> '...*the drama is not tolerated in Geneva. It is not that they disapprove of the theatre in itself; but they fear, it is said, the taste for adornment, dissipation, and libertinism which the actors' troops disseminate among the youth.*' (Rousseau, 1758)

Rousseau suggested remedying this situation by passing strict laws to curb the actors' behaviour, thereby establishing Geneva as a city with 'the advantage of possessing what is thought to be so rare and is so only through our fault: a company of actors worthy of esteem'. This would then avoid, he says, the actors being thought of 'as objects of anathema; our priests would lose the habit of excommunicating them, and our men of the middle class of regarding them with contempt'.

While ingratiating him with the more puritan Genevan bourgeoisie, who took this to mean that he had not relinquished his Calvinist Genevan values, despite being part of French liberal society, his attitude would never be understood by the French thinkers of the time. For the intellectuals of the Enlightenment, this was nothing short of religious oppression.

A Final Break from Geneva

Torn between what Geneva had been and could be, and what it in reality had become, Rousseau felt he could not continue to live there. Yet, paradoxically, he continued to see himself as a defender of his home city and believed that, to be a faithful servant and a patriot, he must defend its rights from outside the city walls (Rosenblatt, 2006).

However, a few years later, in his *Letters Written from the Mountain* (letters written to Christophe de Beaumont and published between 1762 and 1765), Rousseau's attack on Geneva became more open and virulent. Here he responded to the criticism and censorship of his texts, which he saw as a misunderstanding of his thought and therefore unwarranted. He asserted very clearly that there can be no freedom without laws (hence the importance of a well-run state) and also that no one is above the law (criticizing the unchecked power of the Petit Conseil). Rousseau renounced his Genevan citizenship on the 12 May 1763 after the Petit Conseil stopped the sale of the *Letters*.

Learning from an Ancient Historian

Among the classics of Ancient Greece and Rome that Rousseau read with his father, the writer that influenced Rousseau most was the historian and philosopher Plutarch. In a letter to Mme d'Epinay, written in 1756, Rousseau referred to Plutarch as 'my master and my comforter' whose ideas on the republic and virtue Rousseau took up in his writings. In Plutarch's works, Rousseau learnt about the various states in the ancient world and the tales of the great heroes. He saw Plutarch as a moralist and an educator. In *Parallel Lives*, a biography of famous Greeks and Romans which are organized so that their lives are narrated in parallel, Plutarch shows that the virtues of men matter more than their actions.

Reading the classics during his early years shaped Rousseau's moral and political thinking. Throughout his life, he kept to an idealized version of the Roman Republic, a golden age of republican ideals. Throughout his writing, Rousseau commits to a vision of the 'good man' as one who has honour, and is truthful and charitable – these were the qualities of the Roman noblemen and Greek heroes portrayed in Plutarch's writings. (His ideas of a 'good woman' were very different). In his biographies, Plutarch describes Rome as made up of a unified community with common values and common goals who value the good of the city before their own self-interest. Plutarch was also interested in ethics and wrote about the quality of virtue. Following Plato, he defended an education that focused on the development of moral character, not just academic knowledge. This is a theme which would play an important role in Rousseau's treatise on education, *Émile* (see Chapter 5).

Plato's Republic

There is disagreement among academics on just how influential Plato was for Rousseau. Indeed Rousseau himself never acknowledged that he was a follower of Plato and Platonism, perhaps because he considered Plato's vision of knowledge and education to have a degree of elitism. However, Rousseau's nostalgia for the Classical age is clear: in a key passage of the *Second Discourse*, he imagines himself a student of the Lyceum in Athens (a school founded by Plato's student, Aristotle), 'repeating the lessons of my masters, with Plato and Xenocrates for judges' (Rousseau, 1755).

It is also clear that Plato impacted Rousseau's ideas on education to a certain degree – Rousseau saw Plato's *Republic* as the most important treatise on education ever written and would take it as an inspiration for his own treatise, *Émile*. For Plato, education doesn't end in adolescence but is a lifelong pursuit – an idea that Rousseau agreed with and practised. In Ancient Greece, men were educated for the benefit of society: education was centred around teaching someone to become a model citizen, by developing the key virtues of courage, justice, temperance and prudence. In addition, education also involved physical activity, athletics in particular. Rousseau advocates an education in *Émile* which combines physical activity and the understanding of virtue. His aim is to preserve Émile's natural goodness which could easily be corrupted by an unjust and immoral society.

As well as influencing Rousseau's ideas on education, we could argue that Plato also played a part in affecting Rousseau's political idea of a republic. In Book VI of the *Republic*, Plato explains why he thinks representative democracy doesn't work:

politicians are corrupt and self-interested and use rhetoric to win support, and they do not act for the common good. In a striking analogy for how representative democracies work, Plato compares democratic society to a drunken pleasure cruise where the captain is hard of hearing, can't see very well and is kept continually drunk by the crew, who want to get rid of him and take over the ship. The leader of the crew, who helps them take control of the ship from the captain, is praised by them for his cunning and his deviousness, while they refer to everyone outside of their group as 'good for nothing'. The ship has no direction and the crew is only interested in pillage and pleasure. This famous analogy, known as 'the ship of fools', illustrates how representative democracies work: a democratic state cannot flourish if it has no clear direction; elected representatives are only interested in power, and riches cannot help the state flourish. Rousseau is equally critical of representative democracy in *The Social Contract*. As we will see in Chapter 4, elected representatives do not always work in the interest of the people but are more interested in power. Rousseau sees a good society as one where the community matters more than the individual; the downfall of most political systems is that they only benefit the few.

However, this is where the similarities between Rousseau and Plato end, in relation to democracy. Plato advocates a political system where unelected but knowledgeable, skilled leaders – who have the interest of society at heart – rule. Rousseau, however, wants to implement a type of direct democracy. He believes that people should not vote for representatives, but instead vote directly on issues that concern the state: they all, he says, equally represent the state. For Plato a truly just society is one that is run by philosopher kings, people who are educated, rational and knowledgeable about justice and the Good. They are exemplars of moral virtue because they have studied and understood it. In Plato's model of society, the state is stratified in three classes: the philosopher rulers, also called Guardians, who make up the political class; the auxiliaries, or soldiers, who defend the city; and the producers (craftspeople, farmers etc.) who deal with the everyday business of the city. Rousseau disagreed with such a system, built as it was on inequality. Having been brought up in Geneva where the artisans and craftspeople were very well educated and involved in politics, Rousseau had been part of a society that was undervalued by a small patrician council that was scared of giving them too much power. For Rousseau, a good state is one where all citizens are equally involved.

There is, however, a controversial element of Rousseau's political philosophy which may have been inspired by Plato. In *The Social Contract*, Rousseau concedes that there would be a need for a law-maker, or legislator; someone of superior intelligence who helps the citizens of the state to create a sense of collective identity, helps them to make decisions which are for the common good. Rousseau's law-maker – 'the engineer who invents the machine' – is undoubtedly reminiscent of Plato's philosopher kings.

Machiavelli's Anti-monarchism

A key Renaissance thinker who was greatly admired by Rousseau, was Machiavelli (1469–1527), an Italian philosopher known largely for his political ideas and whose works Rousseau read in the original Italian. Rousseau often referred to Machiavelli in his writing, calling him 'an honest man and a good citizen' in a footnote found in the third book of *The Social Contract*. Machiavelli and Rousseau shared a desire to return to Ancient Greek thinking, believing that the political system must be understood separately from the Church, the King or God. Machiavelli was critical of the monarchy because it led to despotism, and of aristocracy because it led to oligarchy. Instead he was in favour of democracy, arguing that, as political decisions affect people's rights, they must share in the political power. He argued that those in power are more concerned with staying in power and preserving their authority than working for the common good. Machiavelli believed that the common good is found in the wisdom of the people, who show better judgment than rulers, and that is why a real consideration of public opinion is important. Rousseau saw in Machiavelli someone who was aware of the dangers of despotism and who trusted ordinary citizens to be better judges; someone who believed that a good government is a republican government which represents the will of its citizens. While Rousseau would argue for a form of direct democracy (rather than a political system where representatives rule on behalf of the citizens), he took from Machiavelli the idea that the will of the people matters and that ordinary citizens are capable of political virtue.

Rousseau the Autodidact

Rousseau's philosophical education and intellectual training began at the age of 16 when he left Geneva and stayed with Mme de Warens. There was little structure and direction to his learning; his knowledge of Greek and Latin came from the seminaries where he was sent to perfect his Catholic conversion. Although he lacked a clear direction, he had high aspirations and liked the idea of developing his intellect, so he read anything he could get his hands on. The following passage from his *Confessions* (Book VI) is particularly illuminating: He writes:

> 'I imagined that to read a book profitably, it was necessary to be acquainted with every branch of knowledge it even mentioned; far from thinking that the author did not do this himself, but drew assistance from other books, as he might see occasion. Full of this silly idea, I was stopped every moment, obliged to run from one book to another, and sometimes, before I could reach the tenth page of what I was studying, found it necessary to turn over a whole library.' (Rousseau, 1782)

He soon developed a clearer method:

> 'On reading each author, I acquired a habit of following all his ideas, without suffering my own or those of any other writer to interfere with them, or entering into any dispute on their utility. I said to myself, "I will begin by laying up a stock of ideas, true or false, but clearly conceived, till my understanding shall be sufficiently furnished to enable me to compare and make choice of those that are most estimable." […] Having passed some years in thinking after others, without reflection, and almost without reasoning, I found myself possessed of sufficient materials to set about thinking on my own account, and when journeys of business deprived me of the opportunities of consulting books, I amused myself

*with recollecting and comparing what I had read,
weighing every opinion on the balance of reason, and
frequently judging my masters.'* (Rousseau, 1782)

Making Contacts in Lyon

With Mme de Warens' financial situation making it difficult for
her to support her young protégé, she found Rousseau work as a
tutor in Lyon in 1739. He was to stay with the de Mably family
and tutor two boys of five and six years of age. Although Rousseau
struggled with his task and found little satisfaction in it, this time
in his life was crucial to the development of his thought. He
found himself surrounded with intellectuals which stimulated
his thinking about human nature, the purpose of education and
the connection between progress and a good state.

Observing the very different characters of his two charges, he
started thinking more carefully about the purpose and methods
of education. More importantly, he soon developed intellectual
friendships with the brothers of his employer. One, the Abbé
de Mably, was writing a treatise on Roman institutions and the
progress of civilization. The other, Étienne de Condillac, studied
philosophy and would later become renowned for his work on
epistemology. Condillac had a huge influence on his contemporary
philosophers, especially those involved in the writing of the
Encyclopedia. What Rousseau learned from him was how to argue
with careful, objective persuasion. He also introduced Rousseau
to other key thinkers, both in Lyon and when he arrived in Paris.

During his time in the de Mably household, Rousseau wrote
two short essays on education for Monsieur de Mably to justify
his educational methods. Some of the key ideas included would

later find themselves in *Émile*. Rousseau argued that children are not simply passive recipients, emphasizing the importance of their active engagement in their learning. He also argued that knowledge of natural sciences is essential, as opposed to the study of Ancient Latin or Greek, which Rousseau didn't see as fundamental to the development of virtuous character.

Rousseau's work in the de Mably household came to an end in the summer of 1741. The next stage of his life, however, was to develop his intellect further. As he arrived in Paris in 1742, he would be witness to the radical intellectual and philosophical movement that was the Enlightenment, and it would prove to be the making of him as a thinker and writer. But before fully immersing himself in this new intellectual world, he spent a year in Venice as secretary to the French ambassador.

Birth of Political Ideas

Rousseau left Paris for Venice in 1743. While he loved the cultural life, developing a passion for Italian music, he was disturbed by the poverty and inequality, and by the poor leadership, dominated as it was by a corrupt nobility. Venice, like Geneva, was a city-state, but whereas the oligarchy in Geneva promoted a tightly controlled industry, growing rich in the process, Venice relied on industry such as gambling and prostitution. While the nobility were protected, the poor grew poorer.

In Book IX of his *Confessions*, he writes:

> *'I saw that everything is connected to politics at its roots, and that from whatever angle one looks at it, a people would never be different from what the nature of their government made them.'* (Rousseau, 1782)

While his political ideas started to take shape in Paris, it was in Venice that he began to understand that every layer of society is tied up in politics. He started thinking about the nature of government and the purpose of the state, and so *The Social Contract* began to take shape. A failing economy meant rising inequality and Venice's political power abroad was waning. He surmised:

> *'it seemed to me that the great question of the best form of government can be reduced to this: "what form of government is suited to forming the most virtuous, enlightened, and wisest people, in short the best people in the largest sense of the word?"'* (Rousseau, 1782)

Rousseau left Venice in the summer of 1744 and after a short stay in Geneva, returned to Paris, where he found work as a tutor. In 1746, he became a research assistant for Monsieur Dupin and his wife, famous in Paris for their literary salon. Monsieur Dupin was working on a critique of Montesquieu's *Spirit of the Laws* (1748), and his wife Louise Dupin was writing on gender equality. In the five years he spent with them, compiling research and making notes, he was obliged to read a multitude of books on politics and history, developing his ideas further for *The Social Contract*.

The Influence of the Encyclopedists

France saw incredible progress in the 18th century, in its industry, architecture and scientific discoveries. But it was a nation dominated by vast inequalities. As an absolute monarchy, it was the nobility who possessed the majority of the land, while the peasants who worked the land were no better than slaves. Furthermore, the Catholic clergy enjoyed enormous privileges, collecting taxes from the poor but paying none themselves. The idea that the King had absolute power over his subjects was increasingly being questioned. It was in this political and cultural climate that a new form of secular philosophy, the philosophy of the Enlightenment, took hold. The Enlightenment refers to a literary, philosophical and scientific movement that took place in Europe in the 18th century. It was grounded in reason, arguing that reason, not faith, should be the foundation of our moral and political thinking. The term 'reason' meant clear thinking that considers logic and critical reasoning, and assumed the possibility of objective truth, untainted by assumptions and bias. Thinkers of the Enlightenment believed that it is prejudices and intolerance which prevent society from progressing; only reason can make mankind progress and flourish, and achieve freedom, knowledge and happiness.

The Enlightenment began with an opposition to established political authorities after the death of Louis the XIV: the King possessed legislative, executive and judiciary powers and therefore total control. The philosophers of the Enlightenment were fundamentally against this form of government. What they also contested were the social inequalities that resulted from this imbalance of power and they set out to fight against what they considered to be a tyrannical governmental system with despots at its head. For them, injustice and ignorance went hand-in-hand, so they argued for political, economic and scientific progress – which they believed would achieve personal and collective freedom. For the Enlightenment philosophers, education and the spreading of knowledge were key to human progress and flourishing. This is why they undertook the task of writing a special form of dictionary that would encompass the sum of human knowledge, including historical as well as contemporary ideas. This they called '*l'Encyclopédie*' (*The Encyclopedia*).

These philosophers also denounced religious fanaticism, the privileges enjoyed by the Church and 'obscurantism' (the lack of critical thought and free thinking). Many of the philosophers of the Enlightenment – including Diderot, Voltaire and d'Alembert – were openly against Catholic dogma. Voltaire, in his short novel *Candide* (1759), showed that blind faith in God in the face of so much human suffering was pointless; it is reason and knowledge, rather than prayer, that can lead us to find meaning and fulfilment in life.

Rousseau met Denis Diderot, one of the driving forces of the movement, in Paris in 1742. Rousseau was initially greatly influenced by his friend Diderot, who was charismatic, sociable and witty. They had a brotherly relationship and were always in competition (though the only thing in which Rousseau bettered Diderot was the game of chess).

Diderot had received more formal education than Rousseau, but he was just as keen to learn new things as his friend, and taught himself English to a level that he was

Fig. 5 Denis Diderot painted by Louis-Michel van Loo in 1767.

able to become a translator. Diderot was a militant atheist who distrusted the Church and argued for greater scepticism. He also wanted a greater democratisation of culture which was one of the rationales behind his greatest accomplishment, the *Encyclopedia*.

As we saw in Chapter 1, Rousseau spent a great deal of time with Diderot, Condillac and d'Alembert. Rousseau saw Diderot as a 'virtuous philosopher whose friendship, already immortalized in his writings, has been the glory and happiness of my life' (quoted in Damrosch, 2007). Their weekly dinners became an indispensable part of Rousseau's development as a thinker and writer, and in Book IV of *Émile* he acknowledges this debt, saying, 'It is the spirit of social gatherings that develops a thinking head and pushes one's vision as far as it can go.' However, Rousseau's thinking would take a different direction to that of his friends, causing an irrevocable split with Diderot in particular.

Rousseau was very much a thinker of the Enlightenment, because he questioned established political systems, defended freedom and equality, and saw the positions of power held by the rich aristocracy as a form of tyranny. But he was also very much at odds with it. He agreed with his colleagues on the *Encyclopedia* that absolutism and fanaticism were an evil but didn't think scientific progress and commerce were the solution. While he played a vital part in the writing of the *Encyclopedia*, penning articles on music and political economy, he didn't think all kinds of knowledge deserved to be pursued, as we saw with his dispute with d'Alembert. Rousseau's understanding of the state was also radically different. As we will see in Chapter 4, in *The Social Contract* he advocated a radical new conception of society and of the role of the State. He disagreed with the thinking of the time that society is the sum of individual self-interest. While he agreed that human beings are naturally self-interested, he argued that self-interest, when it becomes vanity and pride, is detrimental to society and the idea of the common good.

The Philosophy Behind the *Discourses*

Philosophers of the Enlightenment were deeply influenced by the theory of natural law, whose central tenet is that it is essential to understand human nature in order to build a just society where all human beings can flourish.

The question of human nature became central to 17th and 18th century thinking, as philosophers stepped away from a religious understanding of the world. They ceased to believe that nature and humankind's purpose were defined and determined by divine will, and began to look at the world from a secular perspective. They looked at the political implications of a purely rational understanding of humankind, and started rethinking the purpose and functions of the state.

Grotius and Humanism

Natural law, as the basis for political thinking, was brought to the forefront by the Dutch humanist Hugo Grotius (1583–1645) who questioned Catholicism as the foundation for political authority. The aim of natural law theory, he said, was to understand the essence of human nature and derive from it not only moral but also political rules. Grotius argued that human nature is based on two key principles: self-preservation and the need to live in society with other human beings. To achieve a peaceful society, both needs and rights must be preserved and protected. Drawing inspiration from Classical philosophers such as Aristotle and

Cicero, he concluded that political obligations are not God-given (as the Catholic Church would argue), but should instead be derived from our very nature as human beings. Natural law exists regardless of God's existence. While Rousseau was quite critical of Grotius, the idea of a political system grounded in human need and nature, which we find in Rousseau's writings, can be found in the thinking of Grotius and natural law theory.

Burlamaqui's Striving for Happiness

Influenced by Grotius, Jean-Jacques Burlamaqui (1694–1748) was a contemporary of Rousseau and a fellow Genevan. Rousseau draws the substance of his political and philosophical knowledge from Burlamaqui, a legal and political theorist who taught at the academy of Geneva, delivering lectures on ethics and natural law. Essentially, Burlamaqui saw all men in the state of nature as equal: having the same ability to reason, the same capacities and all working towards the same end. He saw all humans as having the same right to pursue peace and happiness, which could be attained by their ability to reason. He also believed in a sovereign body whereby all entrusted his own happiness for the sake of a general happiness within the social body, similar to Rousseau's idea of the General Will. His similarities to Rousseau's thinking here are obvious. However, where he differed was in his belief that a social body could not work without being governed by an enlightened few, who would ensure the successful functioning of an efficient political system, in this way achieving happiness for all.

Burlamaqui's principal message was that what all humans strive for is happiness; this is their primary motivation for action. He also talks about self-love as part of human nature, a concept that

Rousseau would reuse in his *Second Discourse*. What is interesting about his thought, however, is that he sees the purpose of laws not, as Locke and Hobbes argue, as a way to prevent harm, but as a means to make men happy. Burlamaqui's work was to some extent a response to the German philosopher Samuel Pufendorf (1632–94) who argued, like the English philosopher Thomas Hobbes (1588–1679), that a functioning state is one where the government possesses complete power and authority in order to provide security.

While Rousseau took inspiration from natural law theorists in saying that humans, by their very nature, have the right to natural equality, he also believed that to understand the essence of human nature meant considering humans *pre-society*, in a state of nature, as Hobbes and Locke tried to do. Rousseau was convinced that there was something in humankind that is even more fundamental than the ability to reason, and he used the setting of the state of nature to show that humankind, as Burlamaqui had said, essentially strives for happiness.

Social Contract Theorists

Natural law was a common topic among social contract theorists of the 17th and 18th centuries. Their starting point was trying to find a perspective of humans that was outside the realm of political order, and then to find out why a rational individual would choose to be ruled by a political state, rather than live in natural freedom. We will look at this in more detail in Chapter 3.

Pufendorf, Hobbes and Locke had all tried to explain human behaviour within society; they had looked at the type of society human beings should live in, and how they should be governed.

Through a hypothetical thought experiment, they stripped humankind of its social, governed identity and took people back to a state of nature, before they became social animals. They then attempted to answer the core question of why people have consented and still consent to living in a governed state; but beyond that, what are people's political obligations and duties? The state protects them, but what must they do in return?

These philosophers believed every form of social contract (including the one Rousseau conceived of) to be derived from a fundamental understanding of the nature of humankind, which is the starting point for devising a political system. All assumed that humankind must previously have lived in a state of nature outside of society, without laws and obligations. In short, a state of complete freedom. But what was a person like in the state of nature? What drove a human living in this condition? And, more importantly, what happened to make people leave this state to form (and be part of) a political system with laws they would have to obey?

Such philosophical arguments were not meant to be historical narratives of pre-social, primitive humans; rather they were philosophical thought experiments aimed at understanding our place and responsibilities in society.

Hobbes: All Against All

Rousseau came to know the English philosopher Thomas Hobbes during Hobbes's time in Paris, where he became a regular debater in the philosophical circles. There were also many discussions and articles written in the *Encyclopedia* on Hobbism, which naturally Rousseau would have been privy to. Hobbes had been witness to the devastation brought about by the English Civil War (1642–51) which led him to see mankind as inherently selfish and violent. Consequently, Hobbes viewed the state of nature as a state of war – of all against all. In a state of nature, there are no laws and no rights or duties, and in such a state we are all equal. Therefore no one is strong enough to take power. There is no trust in others, and, because of a scarcity of resources, competition and self-preservation would be our main concerns. Hobbes famously referred to the life of humankind in the state of nature as being 'solitary, poor, nasty, brutish and short' in his book *Leviathan* (1651).

According to Hobbes, what drives human beings to create a society are fear and the drive to survive. In a state of nature, people would still be rational enough to realize that living in a group would bring safety and stability. This is the reason that we created a contract relinquishing the many types of freedom we had in the state of nature in favour of an all-powerful figure, which Hobbes called 'the Leviathan'. This figure would initially be the strongest of the group: this person would be the one who could create a coherent group that could be controlled and over which the ruler would act as absolute sovereign. In exchange for protection and a guarantee that they would survive, people would have to obey this absolute ruler. The problem with such a system, Rousseau argued, is that, while it may be warranted in times of war, it gives no rights and no freedom to members of the state.

Locke: Society Brings Security

John Locke, the father of classical liberalism, agreed with Hobbes on grounding society in a social contract, but fundamentally disagreed with Hobbes on his conception of human nature and the basis for a social contract. Locke believed that human beings in the state of nature would be quite content. There would not be a state of 'war of all against all'. Human beings have the faculty of reason, he said, and they are naturally cooperative; they would therefore enjoy the natural rights of life, liberty and property. People in the state of nature are equal and their rights are given to them by God. Why, then, form a contract? Locke thought that becoming part of society is the most rational thing for us to do. Humans in a state of nature would nonetheless be aware that their property and land could potentially be stolen from them, and they might have no means to defend it. If one of their neighbours tried to kill them, they might not be able to protect themselves; in a dispute, there would be no legal system to condemn or defend, no justice and no means to punish. While natural rights are God-given, Locke said, a state could help to protect those rights. In this way, the purpose of a social contract – and the reason that humankind enters into such a contract – is to protect our natural rights. The Constitution of the USA (created in 1789) was very much inspired by Locke's arguments and ideas.

Hobbes and Locke influenced Rousseau's thinking by way of the framework and thought experiments they used in order to understand the state of nature and what political authority should be like. But he disagreed with both of them, and more broadly with the idea of contractualism which was derived from natural law arguments, as we will see in detail in Chapter 3.

Pufendorf: Equal but Different

In *De jure naturae et gentium* (1672), which translates as 'the law of nature and of nations', Freiherr Samuel von Pufendorf laid out his own ideas on what a state of nature would have been like. He disagreed with Hobbes about it being a state of war, instead seeing it as a state of peace. He did however agree that, in a state of nature, human beings are equal and it is this natural equality that gives human beings dignity. For Hobbes, the equality of human beings lies in the fact that they are all equally able to kill each other and that they would rather self-rule than be ruled by others. But Pufendorf understood 'natural equality' as something different. For him, it is the instinctive obligation that all humans have to obey natural law, the innate duties they feel towards one other, and it is what binds them together and makes them equal.

Both Hobbes and Pufendorf, however, believed that there is a degree of inequality in nature, which explains the foundation of the state and the need for a social contract. For Pufendorf, while humans have moral equality, they are physically unequal. Some people are naturally dominant while others are more subservient. Some are more intelligent, some more independent, and some more resilient than others. This ensures that human beings, in their varying abilities and needs, can survive. The unequal distribution of abilities doesn't, however, mean humans are unequal in themselves, as natural law has instilled in humans an innate moral duty to regard others as equals.

Two key concepts dominate Pufendorf's thought: self-esteem and human dignity. According to him, both are God-given rights. Human beings, he said, are aware that they are superior to animals and this is where their dignity lies. God has given animals to humans and has allowed them to be used for human survival. Human beings therefore understand that they can use animals for their needs, but other human beings are equal to them and all have duties towards one another, therefore each must respect the dignity of the other. Human beings also have self-esteem, whereby each individual understands their own particular value and also wants others to appreciate this inherent value. So while human beings may have different abilities, they still understand that they have a duty to regard each other as equals.

How does natural liberty fit in with natural equality? Because human beings have self-esteem, Pufendorf says, they feel they have the natural right to govern themselves and to determine their actions independently of others. No one has authority over anyone else.

The state of nature would evolve into a state where conflict arises, because it is inherently insecure and individual needs would not be met. This is when human beings would realize the necessity of a more formal association: the birth of civil society, of the state, lies in cooperation. Its aim is to formalize a social arrangement. We do not form this association out of selfishness, Pufendorf argues, but out of a desire for friendship. It is about forming a pact, regulating associations, and achieving mutual protection and increasing security.

When the state, or civil society, emerges, a new moral quality arises. Each individual feels a duty of obedience towards society, a recognition of its sovereignty and a moral commitment. Pufendorf's argument is a defence of natural rights (in his case equality) in relation to natural law. In this way, while we may be unequal in civil society, we are still morally equal.

Rousseau disagreed with Pufendorf on a number of things, as we will see in Chapters 3 and 4. However, he did agree with a state of nature not being a state of war, but instead a state of peace, and also with the idea that human beings are naturally sociable. He also took from Pufendorf the distinction between moral equality and physical inequality.

Rousseau's influences are wide ranging: they include places, people, big ideas. While this seems eclectic, there is a thread and a narrative to Rousseau's thought process: his view on human nature and inequality can be traced back to his childhood experiences, to his own experience of inequality and to his witnessing political inequalities. His social contract theory is shaped by his reading of natural law theorists and his short political experience in Venice. His theory of education is influenced by his childhood experiences, but also his reading of Plato and his work as a tutor. Now that we have looked at Rousseau's influences, we need to consider Rousseau's original ideas on human nature, the state and education.

3. Humankind in a State of Nature

Having been exposed to inequality as a fact of life, Rousseau was in a singular position to be able to use his own social marginalization to his advantage. He had experienced and witnessed life on all social levels and was therefore more than qualified to expound his theories on inequality. The idea that inequality is made by people, not God, and that prior to the creation of society, all humans were equal, is something that Rousseau discusses in his *Second Discourse*.

The 'Noble Savage'

Rousseau's philosophy begins with the assumption that humans in their natural state are fundamentally good, uncorrupted by society and living in equality – this is often referred to as 'the myth of the noble savage'. However, to be clear, the word 'savage' doesn't have the same meaning in French as it does in English, and this has caused some misrepresentation over the years as to what exactly Rousseau meant. The French *sauvage* means simply 'natural', not 'barbaric' as has been supposed, and while other English writers did use the term 'noble savage' to refer to a primitive people who they deemed to be barbarous by nature, Rousseau did not.

The term 'noble savage' was a popular concept in Europe well before Rousseau's time and was used as a literary device by social critics to point out the flaws in European culture and to suggest how it might be improved. The discovery of so many lands during the Renaissance period had brought a shocking realization that cultures very different from 'Christendom' existed, and their societies were efficient and harmonious. The idea of the 'noble savage' was first used by French philosopher Michel de Montaigne (1533–92) in his *Essays*. Montaigne considered 'natural man' as 'wild'

> *'... in the same sense that fruits are, produced by nature, alone, in her ordinary way. Indeed, in that land, it is we who refuse to alter our artificial ways and reject the common order that ought rather to be called wild, or savage, in them the most natural virtues and abilities are alive and vigorous, whereas we have bastardized them and adopted them solely to our corrupt taste.*
> (Montaigne, 1580)

Having read Montaigne's works during his time spent in Les Charmettes, Rousseau was greatly influenced by his ideas and they were key to the idyllic vision of the 'noble savage' that Rousseau himself would later adopt. Montaigne argued that, contrary to the idea that a people living without the moral and scientific progress of European colonialists must be cruel, depraved and barbaric, in reality they lived in tune with nature and lead pure lives, free from artifice. This was not purely conceptual, but based on evidence: Columbus had brought seven Arawak-speaking people from South America to the court of

Spain, and Montaigne himself interviewed both travellers and kidnapped Brazilians (Glazier, 1982). People abducted from the 'New World', Ethiopia, Egypt and other non-European lands were housed in a specially constructed village just outside Bordeaux, France (Hodgen, 1964).

Natural Law

Integral to the 17th-century concept of the 'noble savage' was that of 'natural law'. The noble savage was imagined to live in nature according to the governing principles of natural law, to think in accordance with natural reason and to understand God and human creation through natural religion. But what did philosophers mean by 'natural law'?

Independent of human-made laws, the law of nature is understood as being objective and universal, separate from human understanding and from human laws in society. Natural law dictates that people possess an intrinsic sense of right and wrong, which is not taught, but learned – by persistently making morally good choices rather than evil ones. In other words, by using reason.

As we saw in the previous chapter, natural law theorists argued that moral, legal and political systems can be formed from an understanding of human nature, and in this way natural law can be used to build a just society. To do that, they argue, we first need to think about what makes us human. What is universal to all human beings? What do they need, seek, and what makes them flourish? They set out to find an answer from objective research into norms and laws which would apply to all human beings, irrespective of class, culture or society. Natural law theorists wanted to create a universal basis for law, in order to end religious and political disputes.

The History of Natural Law

We find some elements on natural law in Plato and his idea that humans are rational and that a just state must stem from the application of reason, rather than pleasure or custom. It can also be found in medieval Christian philosophy from the 13th century, when St Thomas Aquinas argued that reason, even more than faith, should be the basis of our moral understanding of the world. Aquinas saw reason as central to our understanding of God; faith as well as reason, he argued, can help us understand the world and how to be in it. For Aquinas, the universe, and the human beings within it, had been bestowed with the gift of rationality by God. By following the laws of nature, Aquinas said, which we can work out by using reason, all humans, even non-Christians, are moral.

However, this was natural law understood in the context of religious medieval thinking. For natural law to become secular and universal, an understanding of human nature would first need to go through a more humanist framework. This is what happened during the European Renaissance, which started in Italy in the 13th century. It heralded the rebirth of the Classical values of the ancient world, with a focus on reason, virtue and the pursuit of knowledge and artistic endeavours. The Renaissance was also the start of a humanist movement in philosophy. Renaissance thinkers broke away from medieval scholastic thinking (like that of Aquinas) and the dominance of Catholic thinking on human decision-making. Instead of following divine commands through faith, the humanists wanted to promote the individual and the empowerment of human actions. They argued that human beings have creative powers and agency over their own lives, and that human lives matter in themselves for themselves, and are not just a precondition for the afterlife.

Rousseau and Natural Law

In his *Discourse*, Rousseau combines the language of natural law and the humanist argument around the idea of the 'noble savage' to show that society corrupts. But his true originality lies in the fact that 'he uses the language of natural law against the natural law theorists'. (Rosenthal, 2010)

As we saw in Chapter 2, natural law theorists argued that natural rights are derived from natural law. This is because natural law works as a set of principles, God-given or based on nature, which allow people to survive. Natural law, they argued, is rational, and so human beings have natural rights because they too are rational, even in the state of nature. What Rousseau does is to derive natural law from natural rights, and in a sense turn natural law on its head.

The *Second Discourse*

Rousseau outlined his idea of humans in the state of nature in his *Second Discourse*, which he submitted to the Academy of Dijon in 1754. The question put forward was whether inequality is authorized by natural law. Rousseau didn't win the prize, on the grounds that his essay was too long; but another reason for the Academy's rejection of his work may have been that Rousseau actually identified a problem within the question, and within the notion of natural law itself. Rousseau rejected the idea that humankind has an inherent, unchanging nature centred around reason – instead, he said, a human in a state of nature has the *possibility* to reason, but this faculty isn't yet developed. Rousseau believed that we, as humans, are defined by our ability and openness to change, and with this change comes reason. It is this, Rousseau argued, that would actually be our downfall – and what has led us to inequality. In essence, Rousseau's argument is that nature made humans equal, but society has made them unequal.

Preface to the *Discourse*

Rousseau begins by arguing that it is our ignorance of the nature of humankind that impedes us in creating a true definition of natural rights, which must be relative to inherent human nature. This leads to Rousseau questioning the validity of natural law itself. If we are ignorant of what people in a state of nature are actually like, how are we to determine the natural laws originally prescribed to them? Such a law can only be relevant if 'natural man' is aware of its existence, and besides, it can only be natural if it comes directly from nature itself. These are the questions that Rousseau sets out to consider.

In order to understand the root of inequality, Rousseau argues that it is vital to first make the distinction between a human 'in a primitive condition' and the person that society has produced. Rousseau acknowledges the difficulties of conceiving of humankind in a state of nature that no longer exists (or perhaps, he says, never did exist). The thoughts of a primitive person, he says, are therefore conjecture – a thought experiment – which he sees as the only way to investigate the foundations of human society and ultimately, as we will see in *The Social Contract* (see

Chapter 4), what a good society and a functioning state should be like. Rousseau's critics – Voltaire being particularly vocal on this aspect of his *Discourse* – accused him of advocating a return to the state of nature. However, Rousseau is not disputing that humankind is now a social animal, he is simply arguing that by going back to the origins of humankind in a state of nature and working forwards to find out when and why we created and joined a society, we can begin to understand more about the purpose of the state. In understanding the fundamental nature of humankind itself, we can understand the state we have created, which Rousseau calls 'the true foundations of the body politic'.

Having read voraciously his whole life, Rousseau would have been fully aware that there had been much discussion on the topic already – and plenty of disagreement. The question – what is the nature of humankind? – is central to political and moral philosophy. Philosophers have been arguing for centuries that reason is central to human nature: Aristotle said that 'man is a rational animal'. But for Rousseau, these arguments are based on studying, not humans in a true state of nature, but civilized people stripped of all modern society. For him, this rather defeated the object of understanding *un*-civilized people.

Rousseau argued that there are only two fundamental characteristics of human nature: the first is interest in one's own welfare and preservation (what he calls *l'amour de soi*); the second is repugnance in seeing others suffer or die, an innate compassion or pity for others (what he calls *pitié*). These traits come *before* we develop the ability to reason, Rousseau insists. By the time we begin to use reason, we are no longer in our natural state.

Natural Vs. Moral Inequalities

Rousseau saw the nature of humankind in society as corrupt, violent, and mercenary. He observed two trends in the society he lived in: the violence of the strong and the oppression of the weak. While people in the state of nature are equal, people in society are not. They are driven by the pursuit of riches and the fear of poverty. While it appears that poverty, riches, power and weakness shifts constantly, Rousseau argued that in reality 'the edifice' of society is built on the foundations of inequality.

Rousseau made a distinction between what he saw as two types of inequality: natural inequality, which is physical and to do with our strength, age, gender, body, character, intelligence (something we cannot really change or have control over); and moral and political inequality, which is based on convention (and which we do have control over). Some people have power, riches, privileges and honours, titles and lands, while others are poor, destitute, weaker and therefore powerless – and it is the latter who must obey the former because they lack power to do otherwise. Importantly, Rousseau argued that there is no fundamental connection between these two types of inequalities. Any natural inequalities are transformed by society into political and moral inequalities (see 'Free Will and Perfectibility' later on in this chapter).

Hobbes, Locke and Pufendorf

Rousseau took issue with the false assumption that all humans are naturally equal in terms of capability and morality. As we saw in Chapter 2, his ideas on natural law were influenced by the social contract theorists, Hobbes, Locke and Pufendorf, who understood people in the state of nature as equal, but made inferences about the origins of civil society based on assumptions about the state of nature.

To recap, for Hobbes, the reason why human beings join society under the state is for protection and to achieve peace. For Locke, humans in a state of nature have a rational understanding of their natural rights to life, liberty and property. They join the state because they understand that civil society can protect those rights. For Pufendorf, however, the state of nature is a state of peace, where we have esteem: we value ourselves but also have an understanding of our duties towards others, respecting other human beings' dignity. When the state of nature becomes a state of unrest, we create civil society, he says, in order to establish greater cooperation among men, even though we relinquish some of our freedoms. While men in civil society may not have social equality, they do have moral equality.

But for Rousseau, while these thinkers have set about explaining *how* inequality came about, they do not explain *why*. He argued that each philosopher's definition of morality and human nature reflected their own vision of what society is and should be. Their mistake was 'to consider original man as an intelligent and free being, capable of knowing natural laws and submitting to them voluntarily' (Spector, 2019). Rousseau believed it was absolutely necessary to go back to the drawing board: what is a human like in the most primitive state, and what drove humans in the state of nature (where we could be generally content with our lives and had few desires beyond nourishment and shelter) to join society and experience inequality? For Rousseau, this shift cannot be grounded in notions of protection and justice, as Hobbes argues, or natural rights as argued by Locke and Pufendorf. People in the state of nature have no such awareness. The mistake these thinkers make, Rousseau said, is that they have a conception of the primitive human as a social animal with social needs, including desires and notions of ownership and property, which go well beyond the demands of self-preservation (*l'amour de soi*). Instead, argues Rousseau, we need to think of humankind in a much more embryonic, primitive state.

Humankind in a Natural State

For Rousseau, the differences between humankind in a state of nature or a 'civilized state' are far greater than the differences between primitive people and animals, both of whom share the principles of *l'amour de soi* and *pitié* (by which he means self-preservation and compassion). He imagined humankind in a state of nature to be healthy and robust. Like animals, these people would be attuned to the seasons and living on what was available to them, from a fertile natural landscape that provided fully for all living creatures. Rousseau drew inspiration for this idyllic outlook on narratives of primitive societies in the Americas, as told by merchants and travellers, and documented by Montaigne, and although critics of Rousseau have argued that his notion of 'natural man' is far too idealistic and romantic, his arguments do have some experiential validity.

Rousseau believed that humankind, in a natural state, is amoral, feeling no obligation or duty towards others, and having no sense of right and wrong. This is a major point of disagreement with Hobbes, who thought that a lack of understanding of morality would lead people to be naturally self-interested, and therefore wicked and dangerous. Rousseau, however, draws a very different conclusion: it is *because* people are naturally amoral that the state of nature is one of peace. Self-preservation is not self-indulgence, and it does not incite the capacity for violence; it is society that has created these traits in us.

In a state of nature, humans show aversion to violence and cannot stand to see other creatures suffer, Rousseau asserts. They have a natural compassion and pity, and an innate, instinctual sensitivity which makes them unable to harm others. This natural version of ourselves is similar to that of animals, who tend their young and mourn their dead. Because humans in the natural state are amoral, Rousseau says, they have no real virtues, but this means they have no vices either. Rousseau sees this amorality as a form of natural goodness. Without envy, vanity or contempt for others, there is no desire or need to hurt others. Rousseau disagreed strongly with Hobbes about people's 'natural' fearfulness and instinct to fight. This is not how nature functions, he said: animals do not display viciousness, are not envious of others, and are not unnecessarily aggressive. Humans in a state of nature are just one animal among many, and therefore must function in a similar way.

This is one of the reasons that Rousseau is considered the father of the Romantic movement. For Rousseau and the Romantics, a human is, fundamentally, a sensitive creature who is driven by compassion for others. It is society therefore that has made us selfish and cruel. Rousseau writes in his *Discourse*:

> '*With passions so little active, and so good a curb, men,*
> *being rather wild than wicked, and more intent to guard*

*themselves against the mischief that might be done them,
than to do mischief to others, were by no means subject
to very perilous dissensions. They maintained no kind
of intercourse with one another, and were consequently
strangers to vanity, deference, esteem and contempt.'*
(Rousseau, 1755)

However, there are two important differences between people
and animals in the natural state that caused one to remain in
nature and the other to be drawn out of the state of nature. What
natural man possesses that animals do not is 'free will', which
leads to what Rousseau calls 'perfectibility'.

Free Will and Perfectibility

Rousseau believed that while humans lived in the state of
nature, they were very much like animals, driven by their
instincts of self-preservation. However, whereas animals are
driven by instinct, humans may be driven by, but are not bound
by, their instincts. They possess the capacity to rise above them
– this is what philosophers have traditionally referred to as
demonstrating 'free will'. They show a capacity for
self-improvement, for wanting to live in better conditions.
This is one of the main differences between Rousseau and his
predecessors, who saw human nature as fixed and predetermined.
But Rousseau argues that while animals just *are*, humans have
the ability to become other than what they are at any point
– they can consciously change. A person has the ability to
transform themselves. Rousseau called this ability to change
'perfectibility' and he saw it as key to humankind's change from
being a natural animal to a social one.

This openness to change turned out to be the beginning of our downfall, however. While nature provides fully, we are satisfied; but as soon as it doesn't, we are no longer content. Was this the reason for our change towards forming societies? Rousseau talks of a scarcity of food and of overpopulation as a possibility. He also refers to the birth of the idea of property, which came about very gradually, he notes. As the population increased, humans began to live in closer proximity to one another, began to establish relationships with one another. As they did so, they began to settle, their nomadic lifestyle coming to an end. Leaving the shelter of trees and nature, they began to construct their own forms of shelter, inventing tools with which to construct huts and with which to fish and hunt animals. As humans became more industrious, the idea of property arose. In the second part to his *Discourse*, Rousseau suggests that 'the first man who, having enclosed a piece of ground, bethought himself of saying, "this is mine", and found people simple enough to believe him, was the real founder of civil society'. And with this, Rousseau suggests, came the need to defend and protect his piece of ground from others.

However, Rousseau did not consider property and the wish for a more settled lifestyle as sufficient reasons for people becoming unequal. What was really responsible for this change, he said, was a shift in how humans began to see themselves in relation to others. Once humans began to settle and live closer to one another, their natural physical inequalities would have become more apparent to one another. Differences would perhaps have been perceived in a negative light and would have begun to set humans apart into social hierarchies. As people moved from a natural state into a more socialized one, their sense of love for themselves moved from one form to another; from *l'amour de soi* to *l'amour propre*.

L'Amour de Soi and *l'Amour Propre*

Rousseau drew a very important distinction between these two particular human traits. The first, *l'amour de soi* (love of self), he described as a sort of instinct for self-preservation, as in 'I need to love myself more than I love other things in order to want to survive'. It is linked to pity and compassion because when a 'natural person' sees others suffer, they see their own suffering. This type of love, Rousseau says, is good and is a fundamental trait of a human being living in a state of nature. However, the advent of property and a more settled life gave birth to what Rousseau calls *l'amour propre*, a French term difficult to translate into English, as it is also a kind of self-love, but one based on other people's estimation of us – it is a kind of self-esteem that relies on a comparison of ourselves with others. It is essentially egocentrism, rather than a healthy sense of personal wholeness, and includes a sense of envy and vanity. With *l'amour propre*, a person loves themselves more that they love others and they are envious of other human beings who are stronger or fare better in the world. This is a fundamental trait of civilized people and the root of inequality, Rousseau said. It explains why human beings always desire more, become competitive and ruthless, and stop feeling compassion and pity for others.

Downfall from a Natural State

To sum up, our free will has led us from the contentment of living in a state of nature to the desire for perfectibility; this drew us out of our natural state and conflicts with our natural liberty. In turn, this caused humankind to develop vices and become a tyrant over both other humans and nature. In short, it ensures that we fail to advance *morally*, because we are suppressing our *l'amour de soi* (healthy self-love) and compassion, turning it instead into *l'amour propre* (aggrandizing self-love), in this way creating our own corruption. Therefore, Rousseau argues, it is our capacity for self-improvement, rather than natural law, that created inequality. Originally, people had only physical inequalities, but with our penchant for perfectibility, we began to attach importance to our physical differences, which first created social inequalities and then moral ones. We must therefore have begun to form social institutions and at this point, a new 'state of nature' was established, which was (and continues to be) based on corruption and inequalities.

It was at this moment – of forming societies – that the state of nature became a state of war, as witnessed by Hobbes, and humankind now needs the protection of a state with laws in order to survive. This is why Rousseau sees envy as lying at the core of the change from humankind living in a state of nature to the institution of civil society, as envy is quickly followed by a need to protect what has become 'ours'. The idea of property is central to Locke's argument and has a part to play in Rousseau's also. Both argue that the creation of the state, of the body politic, is made necessary because humans feel the need to protect what they own from others. However, while Locke argues that it is the duty of the state to protect private property, Rousseau believes ownership of private property is the very thing that makes the state corrupt. He isn't against private property, if it is based on needs and on work, but rather the idea of a private owner – how the envious drive for private property has changed humankind.

In Conclusion

What conclusion can we draw from Rousseau's argument in the *Second Discourse*? He argues that inequality is not natural, it is historical; it is the outcome of humankind removing itself from the state of nature. People in the state of nature are naturally good – they have no vices and are complete, independent, free and happy. But when they become part of a society, that natural goodness is replaced with vices. While we were living in a state of nature, pity moderated our self-interest, and pity is really the morality of natural man. In society, it becomes important for us to please others in order to avoid their contempt. The vices we develop in society are illegitimate – they are unnatural because we are alienated from nature. Our natural pity is thus replaced by greed and envy, conventions and laws. But the broader political implications are clear: inequality is the consequence of civic society. There is no natural right to rule, or be ruled, because we are equal in the state of nature. What Rousseau will demonstrate in *The Social Contract*, however, is that it is possible to create a state – a just state – where we rediscover our natural equality and our freedom. Such a state, however, must be based on the consent of the governed.

4. *The Social Contract* and the General Will

The opening paragraph of *The Social Contract* is one of the most famous in Western philosophy:

'Man is born free, and everywhere he is in chains. Many a man believes himself to be the master of others who is, no less than they, a slave. How did this change take place? I do not know. What can make it legitimate? To this question I hope to be able to furnish an answer.' (Rousseau, 1762)

While the society Rousseau described in his *Second Discourse* showed the corrupting nature of society and the state, with inequality based on wealth and power, the aim of *The Social Contract* was to create a new state built on absolute popular sovereignty which he called the General Will, a state which, in his view, would be more just.

Consent is Key

In his *Second Discourse*, Rousseau argued that if a just state was ever to arise it would be one where a common single interest is sovereign; in his dedication to the Republic of Geneva, found at the beginning of his *Second Discourse*, he wished 'to be born in a country in which the interest of the sovereign and that of the people must be identical', where 'the sovereign and the people were one and the same person'. The purpose of the *Second Discourse* was to show why social contracts are a form of alienation, where human beings relinquish their natural freedom and in so doing become alienated. The end of the *Discourse* shares the pessimism of Hobbes: it is the state of war, brought about by the advent of property and the necessity to protect it, that establishes a first contract. While Rousseau's *Social Contract* had a more optimistic vision, he would, however, need to demonstrate that it was possible for a social order to preserve equality and liberty for all. To do so, he would need to redefine the social contract, what authority entails, and what was meant by freedom.

First, Rousseau understood the social contract as an act which makes the state legitimate. For him, it had to be an act of consent based on free association, not an act of submission whereby people appoint themselves a government, as Hobbes had suggested. Instead, it should be a pact, a covenant.

Why join society? For Rousseau, the purpose of political institutions and structures are a way to help humankind regain and retain freedom. Rousseau understood that the conditions for a just state would be difficult to achieve and the state would have to be small and based on equality. But, he argued, a state *could* be just and legitimate if its citizens' political obligation towards the state was based solely on consent.

This is where Rousseau's philosophy becomes truly original. While other political philosophers felt that consent stopped at the stage of the contract itself, Rousseau made it clear that consent is at the heart of a just political institution, and must continue at every stage of politics. This is why, Rousseau argued, it is important to make a distinction between power and authority and to explain what makes the authority of the state legitimate.

Power and Authority

In the first part of the essay, Rousseau explains why previous theories on the legitimacy of the state have been wrong. His main reason for disagreeing with his predecessors is centred around what consent entails.

Rousseau begins by looking at different examples of authority in society and whether they are consensual or forced. Looking first at the authority and obedience that occurs within the society of the family – for Rousseau, 'the only *natural* one' – he compares the father to the ruler and the children to the people. Such a model as this, he says, could surely be called 'the *prime model* of political societies'. However, a father's authority and care for his children is based on his natural affection for them – he protects them and gives them boundaries, which he does through love. But a ruler's authority is not based on affection for his subjects, Rousseau concludes, 'but by the pleasure of being in charge'.

Rousseau next takes up the argument of his predecessors, taking issue with Grotius' words: 'If an individual can alienate [read 'give away'] his liberty and make himself the slave of a master, why couldn't a whole people alienate its liberty and make itself subject to a king?' Rousseau argues that a slave does not *give* himself, but *sells* himself. James McAdam explains what Rousseau means in his essay, 'Rousseau: The Moral Dimensions of Property':

> *'Some may sell themselves into actual slavery (i.e., literal alienation of self) but most do "as good as" because they sell their birthright. [...] In sum, the working poor alienate their bodies, their only property, voluntarily and universally to become the slaves and property of the rich.'* (Parel and Flanagan, 1979)

Rousseau then asks, if a person has sold themselves, what price is being paid? The king reaps benefits from his people – their labour in producing food to feed the country and their toil in keeping the economy going – but what do they get in return? Not peace, Rousseau says, but wars, the 'insatiable greed' of their ruler, and 'harassments by his ministers'.

Aristotle was right, Rousseau argues, when he said that people 'are not naturally equal because some are born for slavery and others for command'. However, for Rousseau, while those born for slavery were indeed born into it, slavery itself is not natural: 'Force made the first slaves', he says, and a state built on slavery is unnatural and unjust. In *The Social Contract* Rousseau maintains his argument that people are naturally free and equal; there may be inequality in health or age, but people are still *morally* equal. No one freely accepts being a slave or being less equal than others. The reason why men may appear to accept a state where some have fewer rights and freedoms than others, and where social structures are unjust, is because society has shaped humans to accept their condition. Remember, that for Rousseau, a human is naturally free but also has perfectibility (see Chapter 2). We are able to adjust to change and fit in with our environment, which is our strength but also our downfall: 'nothing is more certain than that a man born into the condition of slavery is a slave by nature. A slave in fetters loses everything – even the desire to be freed from them' (Rousseau, 1762). But while we may be willing to accept a status of obedience akin to slavery, no such status can ever be legitimate. No one can consent to being enslaved because it is contrary to human nature. A person may submit because they have been habituated to think this is their only possible condition, but this does not make it just. 'If some men are by nature slaves,' Rousseau says, 'the reason is that they have been made slaves against nature. Force made the first slaves; cowardice has perpetuated the species.'

Appeal to Rights

Rousseau has shown that obedience to rulers cannot be made legitimate by appeals to nature. Could it, however, be explained by an appeal to rights? This is what Hobbes argues: the strong, by virtue of their strength, acquire the right to rule. Rousseau argues however, that 'giving way to force is something you have to do, not something you choose to do'. He completely refutes the 'right' of the strongest to rule, explaining that,

> *'If force makes us obey, we can't be morally obliged to obey; and if force doesn't make us obey, then on the theory we are examining we are under no obligation to do so. Clearly, the word "right" adds nothing to force: in this context it doesn't stand for anything.'* (Rousseau, 1762)

Hobbes' social contract attempted to make the power of the strong legitimate; through the contract, their power is inscribed in law and citizens have a duty to obey. Rousseau, however, argues that no power dependent on the strong dominating the weak can be legitimate. He writes that 'however strong a man, he is never strong enough to remain master always, unless he transforms his Might into Right, and Obedience into Duty' (1762). As argued above, absolute obedience is a form of slavery and no one can ever legitimately have absolute authority over another.

For Rousseau, a just state is one grounded in the consent of its citizens. That consent is explicit and, as we will see later on in this chapter, grounded in the ability that citizens – as a whole – have to express their will, which Rousseau calls the General Will. That means citizens are free because their consent doesn't stop once the contract is established; the contract presupposes that they are always in a position to consent.

However, the role of a good state should not just be to guarantee freedom, Rousseau says; a good state should be just and therefore virtuous. Politics and morality cannot be distinguished. Rousseau wanted to show that political institutions can be virtuous and that it is possible to overcome the evils of civil society as we know it. The *Second Discourse* made it clear: society corrupts humankind and turns people towards vices. Society makes us selfish and contemptuous, and strips us of our self-esteem and dignity. Society is rooted in and promotes inequality. But we cannot go back to a state of nature, because the amorality of the 'noble savage' is gone; still, as social beings we have a moral dimension and the potential to be virtuous.

How then, do people come to form a state? Rousseau proposes that the social contract must start with a surrender; people must surrender their individual authority to the General Will. Rousseau rejected the notion of God-given sovereignty and believed that this would only be possible in a Republic. These ideas were revolutionary at a time when France and other European countries were ruled by absolute monarchies and when the power in the Republic of Geneva was held by a group of rich families.

So how does Rousseau succeed in reconciling the initial surrender of natural freedom when people join the state with his argument that the state should guarantee freedom? He solves this apparent contradiction by redefining the very concept of freedom.

Positive and Negative Freedom

The formal distinction between positive and negative freedom is a modern one, usually associated with the philosopher Isaiah Berlin (1909–97), who introduced the distinction in his 1958 lecture, 'Two Concepts of Liberty'. 'Negative freedom' refers to freedom from constraint; the 'negative' referring to an *absence* of something (obstacles, constraint, interference from others). Whereas positive freedom refers to the *presence* of something, such as self-control, self-determination, or self-mastery, for example. Berlin explained it like this:

> *'The first of these political senses of freedom [...] I shall call the "negative" sense, is involved in the answer to the question "What is the area within which the subject – a person or group of persons – is or should be left to do or be what he is able to do or be, without interference by other persons?" The second, which I shall call the positive sense, is involved in the answer to the question "What, or who, is the source of control or interference that can determine someone to do, or be, this rather than that?"'*

(Berlin, 1969)

Essentially, the difference between these two concepts is the involvement of external and internal factors: the external interference one suffers (negative) and the internal factors affecting one to act autonomously (positive). Socialism advocates limited negative freedom in favour of positive freedom, that is the freedom to achieve our potential, but that implies some government intervention. Rousseau (and modern socialists) tend to privilege positive freedom at the expense of negative freedom. While Rousseau never formalized the distinction between negative and positive freedom, modern thinkers tend to reflect on his argument through that helpful distinction.

According to Rousseau, in order to be part of civil society, we must give up our natural freedom ('freedom from', so a negative freedom) in order to gain political freedom which, for Rousseau, consisted of civic and moral liberty (which are forms of positive freedom). Contrary to thinkers such as Locke, who argued that the state protects our natural liberties, understood as rights (to property, life and liberty), Rousseau argued that political freedom is more than the protection of rights.

Remember that, for Rousseau, while people have natural freedom, they do not have natural rights. Rights are given by the state. But in order to acquire such rights there must first be a redefinition of freedom. For Rousseau, freedom is not freedom from constraint, but rather freedom to become a rational being, which involves recognizing that one person's freedom is limited by, and should not encroach upon, the freedom of others. This sort of freedom is a political freedom and is given by the sovereign state, which as we will go on to see, is made up *of* the people *for* the people. This political freedom is consistent with Rousseau's idea of our instinct for self-preservation (from healthy self-love, *l'amour de soi*) which, as we saw in the previous chapter, is linked to compassion towards other beings. In this way, Rousseau says, 'the two contracting parties – the individual member and the body politic – are obliged by duty and by self-interest to give each other help.'

Modern critics see Rousseau as defending a form of positive freedom. Rousseau saw that in an unjust state the poor cannot flourish, which is why equality is necessary – an equality which involves measures to prevent disparity in riches, and has a strict state control of property. Liberals have argued this is not freedom at all because it comes with too many restrictions, preventing citizens from having the power to choose and do as they wish. Rousseau, however, saw his redefined concept of freedom through the lens of perfectability: by *becoming* the sovereign, human beings are free to fulfil their potential.

Moral Freedom

Rousseau was not only advocating a form of positive freedom that allows people to remain equal. The purpose of the state is also to make us moral beings. Rousseau professes that a third type of freedom exists, which he calls 'moral freedom'. This is freedom to obey a law that we give ourselves, he says, which does at first appear to be self-contradictory. However, when humans join together to form a society or state they are no longer 'noble savages': they are more rational; family bonds are more intricate; they invent agriculture and industry, and own property. Being part of that state requires a change in how humans view themselves and others. They must be ready to recognize that joining the state is necessary not only for their self-preservation but for the preservation of others; it is love for oneself and for others (*l'amour de soi*) that enables this entry into Rousseau's civil society.

Critics argue, however, that Rousseau demands complete alienation: that joining the state involves relinquishing all our rights and individuality; that we have to give ourselves completely to the state. Rousseau admits that in order to gain freedom in the state one must accept severe limitations – how much property one can own for example. But this, for Rousseau, is just the sacrifice of natural liberty. All are equally alienated as members of the state; all gain equally. He writes: 'since each has made surrender of himself without reservation, the resultant conditions are the same for all: and, because they are the same for all, it is in the interests of none to make them onerous to his fellows.' (Rousseau, 1762)

Therefore, while man may abandon his natural freedom, he gains greater freedom: political and moral freedom. But does it make sense in relation to individual rights? And does it mean the state have a say in citizens' private matters? Rousseau clarifies his position with his concept of the General Will.

General Will and Individual Will

The idea of the General Will is connected to Rousseau's concept of *l'amour de soi* (healthy self-love). He does not see the General Will as the will of the majority, or even an aggregate of individual wills. Instead, he argues, it must be an association which involves social bonds. It is the way individuals become a people or, as Céline Spector puts it in her book *Rousseau* (2019), 'the real contract is a pact of association by which a multitude becomes a people, not a pact of submission by which people give themselves leaders.' Robert Nisbet, in his 1943 paper on Rousseau, explains it even more succinctly: 'The General Will is the analogue of the human mind, and as such must remain as unified and undiversified as the mind itself.'

Rousseau sees the General Will as a singular entity and therefore tends to refer to it as though it were an individual. As no individual can be enslaved by laws they themselves have created, the social contract cannot force laws on the General Will. Conversely, the citizens that make up the sovereign – the General Will – are bound to both the sovereign (as individuals) and to other individuals (as the sovereign).

Therefore it is in each individual's best interest to think of the common good, not just their own particular interest. The General Will rests upon humans understanding and accepting their duties in the state. It is a voluntary contract based on consent, whereby all citizens make the laws and obey the laws. The law itself is intended to protect the whole community, not particular groups, thus guaranteeing equal rights. Each individual is thus part of the General Will and *is* the General Will.

The sovereignty of the General Will is absolute, Rousseau says. It cannot be split apart, nor a position within it be relinquished. He writes: 'for the same reason that sovereignty is inalienable, so, too, is it indivisible, for either the will is general or it is not. Either it is the will of the whole body of the People, or it is the will merely of one section' (Rousseau, 1762). The will of the individual is therefore dangerous because it can so easily conflict with the General Will, which is why Rousseau stressed the need to give up individual freedom. In this way, the General Will can prevent inequality, the forming of groups through institutions, and the prevention of freedom through force or privileges.

Rousseau has been criticized for inciting modern totalitarianism. However, such an accusation is anachronistic as, far from wishing to create an authoritarian state, Rousseau placed emphasis on a state based on consenting citizens making their own laws for the good of all. He wanted to turn *l'amour propre* (envious egocentrism) of people back to a sort of collective *l'amour de soi* (healthy self-love). In his most controversial passage in *The Social Contract*, in Book I, Chapter VII, Rousseau says,

> *'In order then that the social compact may not be an empty formula, it tacitly includes the undertaking, which alone can give force to the rest, that whoever refuses to obey the general will shall be compelled to do so by the whole body. This means nothing less than that he will be forced to be free; for this is the condition which, by giving each citizen to his country, secures him against all personal dependence. In this lies the key to the working of the political machine; this alone legitimizes civil undertakings, which, without it, would be absurd, tyrannical, and liable to the most frightful abuses.'*
> (Rousseau, 1762)

While this does indeed sound totalitarian, the key to understanding what Rousseau really meant is to understand what he means by 'freedom'. Robert Nisbet, in his study 'Rousseau and Totalitarianism', explains:

'What gives uniqueness to Rousseau's doctrine is not so much its severity as its subtle but explicit identification with freedom. What has connoted bondage to the minds of most men is exalted as freedom by Rousseau. To regard the power structure of the state as a device by which the individual is only being compelled to be free is a process of reasoning that sets Rousseau apart from the tradition of liberalism.' (Nisbet, 1943)

Remember that Rousseau is very much against society in its modern form – a society that he sees as unjust and unequal. By forcing man to be free, the General Will is emancipating him from a traditional (discordant) society. As Nisbet puts it: 'Through the power of the state, man is spared the strife and tyranny which arise out of his selfish and destructive passions.' One could argue then that, paradoxically, it is when *l'amour propre* (egotistical self-love) steps in that men abandon their (political and moral) freedom.

Unfortunately, however, Rousseau's ideas were misused by some of the leading figures of the French revolution and its immediate aftermath, The Terror, when members of the aristocracy, the clergy and political opponents were ruthlessly killed. Rousseau would have been the first to condemn such actions. He believed that laws should bind citizens together; that by each individual actively participating in the laws of the state – in civil freedom – each is free to determine their own fate.

It is important to remember, too, that Rousseau's purpose in creating the social contract was to create a harmonious state where there is social justice, where people are treated equally and with respect. The inequality created by absolute monarchies, and by economies driven by money and property, cannot achieve that. In these forms of state, freedoms are not sacrificed for the good of the whole. Summarizing Rousseau's argument, Joshua Cohen, in his book *Rousseau: a Free Community of Equals*, says:

> *'In the society of the general will, citizens share an understanding of the common good and that understanding is founded on the members' commitment to treat one another as equals by refraining from imposing burdens on other citizens that those members would be unwilling to bear themselves.'* (Cohen, 2010)

However, do private family interests fall into the same bracket? Rousseau is careful to make clear that the General Will is not an arbitrary force, it isn't tyrannical, and therefore has no business in its citizens' private life. While individuals are expected to make decisions that impact the life of the community positively, and not merely for their own private interests, the community can only expect that which is necessary from the individual and they are only bound to the sovereign in matters that concern the community as a whole. The motivation to put society and community first is what Rousseau sees his *Social Contract* as striving towards, seeking to make man a more moral being.

Generating Legislation

Rousseau goes on to consider how the laws would be made. The sovereignty of the state, and so (automatically) of its citizens, lies in its ability to legislate – to make and implement laws – and the law must be the expression of the General Will.

Laws are derived from the contract; each citizen, as they deliberate on the enactment of a law, must ask themselves whether it preserves freedom, equality, and the spirit of the contract. Any law that undermines these is void. They must also ask themselves, not whether the contract is in their self-interest, but whether it preserves the sovereignty of the people and conforms to the General Will and the body politic. If they feel it would be a burden, they need to consider whether it would be a burden for all of society, not just for themselves. For example, if a citizen is concerned about heavy taxation and how it would affect their personal finance, they should consider, too, if that burden also falls on all other citizens but would benefit society as a whole. In this sense, for Rousseau, laws are expressions of our individual freedoms but also our collective freedoms.

Rousseau defines legitimate laws as those that guarantee equality and fairness; no individual should have more rights or enjoy the benefits of the state more than others. No one is above the law, he says. The law must reflect the interest of all its members while securing each individual's autonomy. However, how can a people all sit down together and decide a law unanimously? After all, people don't always know what is best for them, or even what they want. Rousseau proposed the following:

'Individuals must be made to bring their wills into line with their reason; the populace must be taught to know what it wills. If that is done, public enlightenment leads to the union of understanding and will in the social body: the parts are made to work exactly together, and

*the whole is raised to its highest power. For this there has
to be a law-maker.'* (Rousseau, 1762)

The Role of the Law-maker

Rousseau acknowledges that, while citizens may be willing to freely assemble as a single body and decide collectively, they will likely struggle to create just laws and reach the right judgment. To help and guide citizens to draft a consensual constitution, Rousseau proposes the solution of an enlightened individual who will act as the foundation of the nation. This individual takes the form of a *legislateur*, or law-maker – a person of superior intelligence, great insight, unbiased, and willing to work selflessly on behalf of all citizens. These requirements mean that the law-maker cannot be a citizen of the state. Rousseau admits that such 'an individual and superior role [...] has nothing in common with human power' and that 'It would take gods to give men laws!' Rousseau's law-maker does not, and cannot, take the form of a legislator, political leader, judge, or even dictator, in the way that we might understand it. Instead this supreme being is someone who devises a moral code which will create a better people. Therefore, if we follow Rousseau's logic, morality is derived from rationality; human's capacity for rationality has led to the creation of civil society; and civil society is enabled by the law-maker. Rousseau sees the law-maker as an enlightened moral guide who can help citizens reach civic and moral virtue.

The law-maker is, however, a controversial figure in Rousseau's philosophy. To some, he appears at times to be a despotic figure, but for Rousseau he is a being of a higher nature than humans:

'What the legislator puts into the mouth of the immortals are decisions based on a high-flying reason that is far above the range of the common herd, the aim being to constrain by divine authority those who can't be moved by human prudence.' (Rousseau, 1762)

The law-maker does not rule by force or reason, but instead takes on a third type of authority: the divine, which, Rousseau says, 'can constrain without violence and persuade without convincing', that is to say, get people to agree without resorting to reasoning. He gives Calvin as an example of a legislator as well as Lycurgus and Moses; all, said Rousseau, were divinely inspired and sought the common good.

But can such a state exist? Rousseau saw himself as a potential *legislateur*, drafting constitutions for Corsica (1764) and Poland (1791). Yet, the conditions for such a state to exist are very strict; it must be small, there can be no factions, no pressure from oligarchs, associations or lobbies, and no political parties. Also, each citizen must vote on their own accord, something that, even in a city-state such as Geneva, would be difficult to enforce. Rousseau's *Social Contract*, while something of an ideal, remains a paradigm against which to measure other forms of government. Even Rousseau concedes that 'There never was and never will be a real democracy in the strict sense of the word.' (*The Social Contract*, Book III, Ch. IV)

But what about the citizens themselves? According to Rousseau the ideal citizens of his ideal state must be well informed and educated. This is where his treatise on education, *Émile*, comes in.

5. On Education

Rousseau published his work on education the same year he published *The Social Contract*, both of which can be understood in the broad framework of his system of thought. *Émile* or *On Education* was essentially a revolutionary hybrid novel/treatise on educational reform which became infamous for undermining education – especially moral education – as it was perceived at the time. As religious education was expected to begin at around the age of six, Rousseau's philosophy was seen as a threat to the authority of the Church. Rousseau rejected the blind acceptance of religious traditions and principles and instead advocated the use of reason when practising moral judgment. This is what makes Rousseau a philosopher of the Enlightenment, although he was unique in that – unlike Diderot and Holbach, and other philosophers who were staunch atheists – he maintained his belief in God, finding blasphemy repugnant. Mme d'Epinay recalled Rousseau's utter of indignation one evening at dinner when he exclaimed: 'If it's cowardly to speak ill of one's friend who is absent, it's a crime to speak ill of one's God, who is present. As for me, *messieurs*, I believe in God.' (quoted in Damrosch, 2007) Rousseau was not, however, afraid of criticizing the church, as is apparent in the most controversial passage in *Émile* – 'The Profession of Faith of the Savoyard Vicar' – which led to the book being banned and even burnt in both France and Geneva.

Treatises on education follow a philosophical tradition which dates back to Plato, the nature and purpose of which are very much part of philosophical endeavours. Rousseau acknowledges Plato's influence but his theory of education is also deeply influenced by empiricist philosophy and Locke's view that the mind is a *tabula rasa* (blank slate at birth).

For Rousseau, the purpose of education is not to inform or instruct, but to form a person's character while preserving their innate natural goodness. Its aim is to make children moral beings who are happy and content, beings who understand the true meaning of self-interest but also care for, and have compassion for, others. Although Rousseau was under no illusion that the natural state of humankind that he described in his *Second Discourse* could realistically exist in his present-day society, he did believe that it would be possible for man to maintain the virtues of *l'amour de soi* (healthy self-love) while living by the obligations of the 'contract' required by society. By writing *Émile*, in the form of a philosophical treatise on education, Rousseau set out to show how this was possible.

Educating Émile

Émile was not a real child, but a fictional one that Rousseau created for the purpose of his work. As with his *Second Discourse*, Rousseau's treatise on education, *Émile*, is very much a thought experiment, focusing on the ideal upbringing a child should have, which includes strict criteria: Émile must be an orphan, be raised in the countryside away from the corrupting influence of city folk; and he must come to his tutor as a new born, as Rousseau believed that education should start from birth. He must be rich (Rousseau, rather controversially, argued in *Émile* that the poor do not need an education, nor do girls – other than 'how to manage their house and look after their family'). He must also be in excellent health (the teacher should not waste his time on an unhealthy child who may be at risk of dying or who never develops the moral and rational faculties to progress as should be wished). The boy must stay with his teacher until he gets married and becomes a father; his education will allow him, in turn, to raise his child well. For Rousseau, Émile is a male child who can be educated and, in a sense, have his humanity saved in the current corrupt society. Remember that, for Rousseau, human beings are naturally good and it is society that corrupts them, starting with education. In order to save the young Émile from society, Rousseau isolates him from others.

What did Rousseau deem to be wrong with the education system as it was in his day? He believed that children were alienated from themselves to become what a corrupt society wanted of them; similarly to what he argues in *The Social Contract*, Rousseau perceived social human beings as being alienated from their essential being, each person being reduced to a cog in the machine that is society.

Each chapter of the book concentrates on a specific age period which Rousseau considered significant and which he believed required a different method. The aim however was to teach Émile to live a good life and to flourish.

Books I & II

The first stage of education, The Age of Nature, covers the first two years of the child's life, a time that Rousseau believed should be spent with the mother or nurse maid. At the time when wet nursing in rich families was the norm, Rousseau argued that breastfeeding was essential to the bonding of a child with its mother. He saw babies and young children as very much like animals, and emphasized the importance of them being free to run and explore and move, arguing against swaddling babies as it restricted their natural movements. For Rousseau, swaddling young infants is the first method society uses to shape and dominate children.

The second stage in The Age of Nature takes place between the ages of two and twelve. Here Rousseau outlines the law of necessity: while a child must not be neglected, it is important not to abide by all their demands to the point where they become a tyrant. What children need to learn is independence, rather than reliance on others; they need to be able to fulfil their own needs and be self-sufficient. A child needs to learn to seek help when needed but not become imperious, which Rousseau sees as the first step towards vice and corruption (and thus *l'amour propre*, an egotistical self-love). There should be no excessive punishments and the child should not be made to obey commands. Rousseau recommends no formal teaching; instead instruction should focus on the child discovering their surroundings, learning to interact with objects. The tutor should respect the child's freedom and allow them to take risks, encouraging physical games.

Émile is neither taught to read nor to write. He is taught no languages, history or geography, and he is not taught to learn poems by heart (a very common practice in France even today). He is also not educated in morality. What matters first and foremost, at this early stage, is his physical wellbeing, encouraged through physical education, and his interaction with nature. This idea is a conceptual echo of the time that Rousseau spent in Bossey and the discovery of his love for nature and botany. In his treatise, Rousseau goes on to advocate that the child should have a small plot where they are able to grow plants in the garden, an activity that Rousseau clearly saw as an important part of his own emotional development as a child.

This outline for an early education that excluded study is what Rousseau called 'negative education', which aimed to prevent the development of vice by letting a child develop independence on the basis of their natural freedom. Positive education, which Rousseau rejected, is traditional education as we know it, with a focus on formal learning. Young children being asked to learn times tables or poetry through rote learning in primary schools is an example of positive education; similarly, assemblies based around religion or moral behaviour are also forms of positive education. For Rousseau, this sort of education serves only to corrupt rather than educate. It shapes children into what society wants them to be, rather than treating them as autonomous individuals with the capacity to flourish on their own.

Book III

The third part of *Émile*, The Age of Strength, focuses on boys between the ages of 12 and 15, as they go through adolescence. And it is here when a more formal education begins. The role of the tutor, Rousseau proposes, is to make the child curious. He makes a distinction here between subjects that are useful and others which are less so. For example, a study of nature is important, as is astronomy, but it must be taught in context; a lesson in astronomy may arise while watching a sun set or a full moon. However, Rousseau still does not advocate learning history at this stage, and in fact recommends very little reading. He sees it as important to read only what the child is curious about, which will make learning more exciting to the child and, essentially, encourage him to educate himself. He recommends books such as *Robinson Crusoe*, which he sees as a lesson in survival, living in tune with nature and being resilient. It teaches that nature can be punishing at times and dangerous, but that it is something that sustains man and therefore deserves respect. The Bible, on the other hand, he rejects outright, saying that it teaches man to fear God and to follow tradition, something that Rousseau was against at all costs. It is at this stage in a child's life, that Rousseau believes they are able to develop their own capacity to reason. Therefore, with the careful guidance of the tutor, books should be suggested which correspond to the child's individual characteristics and nature.

Book IV

The final stage, The Age of Reason and Passions, takes place between the ages of 15 and 20, and is a time for Émile to discover his heart, make him understand what love is, and allow him to enter society, which is unavoidable. It is also in this final section – Book IV – where we find what was conceived to be the truly scandalous passage of *Émile*: The Profession of Faith of the Savoyard Vicar. Here Émile is introduced to the idea of God and religion for the first time. Instructed through the narrative of the Savoyard Vicar, Émile is taught to look at religion through the eyes of a sceptic – to be a freethinker and discover for himself how truly glorious God is, rather than being indoctrinated by the Church.

In this part of the text, Rousseau reasserts his view that 'evil' is essentially moral evil that is created by people. God did not create evil but, by giving people their freedom, He has given humans the ability to allow evil to exist. People are responsible for choosing good over evil. Nature is fundamentally good, Rousseau

Fig. 6 Émile and the Savoyard Vicar in an etching created by Jean-Michel Moreau in 1777 for *Émile*.

writes, but it is man who destroys it. This text very much made Rousseau a dissident and regarded as the enemy of Rome. Although pious in his own way, Rousseau always followed his heart and his conscience, putting his beliefs before religious institutions and dogmas, which for him were corrupt and corrupting. For Rousseau, religious doctrine acts to enslave mankind, prevents people from thinking freely, and essentially sells a lie – whereas nature never lies. We will look at the Savoyard Vicar's teachings in more detail later on in the chapter.

Book V

In the fifth book, The Age of Wisdom and Marriage, Rousseau focuses on the education of girls through the lens of Émile's future wife, Sophie. Rousseau creates the character of Sophie as the perfect woman and as perfectly compatible with Émile. The aim of her education, however, is not to develop reason and judgment, as it is for Émile, but instead focuses on teaching her to please and to be subservient, as well as how to accomplish domestic tasks. Rousseau has been strongly criticized over the years for his sexual politics, and *Émile* is no exception. For the modern reader it is shocking to see such clearly defined gender roles whereby Rousseau's Sophie exists only in relation to Émile. Interestingly, there have been several feminist writers who have approached *Émile* from different standpoints. Penny Weiss, in *Gendered Community: Rousseau, Sex and Politics* (1993), makes a case for Émile being far less free than he appears, and Sophie being far less enslaved. She argues:

> '*Establishing the important similarities and connections between the educations of women and men allows for a more coherent interpretation of Rousseau's work. Both sexes are acknowledged to go through various developmental stages that must be respected in education. For both, the limits and wonder of childhood are respected, and both are taught that which will be useful in their (different) adult lives. Each is given both sensitivity to opinion and some means of resisting it. Both are resourceful, neither is self-sufficient.*' (Weiss, 1993)

Rosanne Kennedy (2012) suggests that Book V is ironic and that the voice of the tutor is not that of Rousseau, rendering this section of *Émile* a critique of the two diverse educational methods. Kennedy argues that to read Book V as sincere is implausible, particularly as 'it is preceded by an absolutely contrarian ideal at the end of Book IV, in which an alternative utopia critical of not only the patriarchal family but all relations of authority and domination, is put forth.' Here, Kennedy is referring to the section which reads,

> *'There I would gather round me a company, select rather than numerous, a band of friends who know what pleasure is, and how to enjoy it, women who can leave their arm-chairs and betake themselves to outdoor sports, women who can exchange the shuttle or the cards for the fishing line or the bird-trap, the gleaner's rake or grape-gatherer's basket. There all the pretensions of the town will be forgotten.'* (Rousseau, 1762)

Educational Reform

Some of the content may appear controversial, and quite strange at times, to the modern reader, but Rousseau was writing for the people of his time: the middle classes and the aristocracy who were sending their children to boarding schools or educating them at home with the help of a tutor. Children at school were often beaten and abused, spent most of their time learning their lessons through rote without really understanding what they were learning, or were taught rhetoric in order to converse in polite society. Rousseau found the education of children at the time to be both damaging and full of contradictions. It focused on self-interest but attempted to foster the values that made boys into male citizens. Children were taught about morality but the lessons in question only reflected the accepted values of the time and lacked authenticity.

While *Émile* may initially appear to be a treatise on education, it is a lot more than that: it focuses on the raising of a man in a domestic setting, but the text has a profound political dimension. Rousseau is setting up an education system which would be the foundation of a sound political system. Although Rousseau advocated a private and solitary education for Émile, this is because the social conditions for a state education were not present. In his view, the education children received at the time did not follow a natural order, that is, one which starts with the development of the senses, is followed by the development of reason, and therefore by the development of virtues and love for others. A good education is one where *l'amour de soi* doesn't become corrupted into *l'amour propre*. Rousseau's 'natural education' is not one where children are left to their own devices, nor is it one which condones a return to the state of nature. A proper education, he argues, is one where the tutor allows the pupil to develop his senses through a range of experiences and his own judgment only at the point when he displays the intellectual capacity to do so. Such an education is in tune with nature.

The Savoyard Vicar

Émile's tutor tells the story of a young Italian man he met 30 years ago, a man who was morally lost and had faced exile. This man had met a priest (the Savoyard vicar) who took him on and made it his mission to rekindle his natural goodness. It turns out that this young man is in fact the tutor himself.

It is quite probable that Rousseau wrote this section as an independent piece which he then inserted into *Émile*, as it is written in quite a different way to the rest of the book. The text is very theoretical and sits in stark contrast to most of Émile's education, which is more practical. Here Rousseau deals with metaphysical questions, such as: What is the mind? What is God? What is the nature of evil? Critics such as Céline Spector have argued that Rousseau is in fact outlining his own thinking on more theoretical questions through the voice of the vicar, who is a combination of two priests Rousseau met when he was younger, at the time he was trying to convert to Catholicism: Abbé Gaime in Turin and Abbé Gatier in Annecy.

The vicar is a simple man, the son of a peasant whose parents encouraged him into a life of the Church. However, he never found solace or meaning in the Church nor in the works of philosophers, where he sought truths that would allow him to lead a better life. Having broken his vow of celibacy and been excommunicated, the vicar rejected his Christian faith and began to search for his own truth.

He first clarifies why he re-examined his principles and assumptions, using a method not dissimilar to the philosopher René Descartes in his *Meditations on First Philosophy* (1641). This involves suspending judgments on everything that could possibly be false until one arrives at a fundamental, infallible truth. The Church, the vicar says, asks for absolute submission but this means depriving followers of the use of their judgment and reason. While Descartes asserts the fundamental truths of reason, the vicar, after much soul searching, believes he must follow his conscience not his reason. He argues that the only possibility of knowledge is through the senses. The only way we can know ourselves is by examining our experiences given to us by our senses. He says:

> *'I am not, therefore, a mere sensitive and passive, but an active and intelligent being; and, whatever philosophers may pretend, lay claim to the honor of thinking. I know only that truth depends on the existence of things, and not on my understanding which judges of them; and that the less such judgment depends on me, the nearer I am certain of approaching the truth. Hence my rule of confiding more on sentiment than reason is confirmed by reason itself.'* (Rousseau, 1762)

The influence of Locke and Condillac here is clear. We cannot detach ourselves from our bodies and our senses; all our claims of knowledge stem from our initial sensations. No metaphysical truth exists which we know innately or can grasp a priori through reason. However, this doesn't make the vicar (or Rousseau) an empiricist: he will argue against materialism (the view that only physical substance exists) in order to prove theism (the belief that God exists).

The vicar (through Rousseau) argues that although the universe is material and governed by the laws of physics, one can derive from observing the world that there is a God who created it. No object moves itself and the universe could not have created itself. A will must therefore have created the world and the laws of nature; nature itself shows purpose and order and only a divine will can explain this. The vicar makes it clear that this itself is not proof of God's existence but instead an intuition gathered by what he sees of the world (in other words, through his senses). Objects in the world show order, design and purpose, nature is organized and shows perfection, which only a divine being could have created. However, he feels that there is not much more he can claim to know about God and he only knows of God through that which He has created. While God is eternal, pure cognition, a creator who is just and benevolent, human understanding is limited. This is why knowledge of God cannot be solely derived from reason or from experience. We really know God through religious experience, that is, a subjective, personal experience which allows us to gain awareness of God's existence.

Through this argument Rousseau shows that he disagrees with natural theology, which attempts to prove the existence of God solely from reason or experience, as opposed to religion. At the same time, the fundamental truths discovered by the vicar are not philosophically known truths; they are truths which every human has access to. In the following passage, Rousseau argues that the existence of God can be proved through religious experience. What is key to this argument is that organized religion, through books and religious leaders, is not necessary in order to have knowledge of God. Rousseau declares:

> *I believe, therefore, that the world is governed by a wise and powerful Will. I see it, or rather I feel it; and this is of importance for me to know. But is the world eternal, or is it created? Are things derived from one self-existent principle, or are there two or more, and what is their essence? Of all this I know nothing, nor do I see that it is necessary I should. In proportion as such knowledge may become interesting I will endeavour to acquire it: but further than this I give up all such idle*

*disquisitions, which serve only to make me discontented
with myself, which are useless in practice, and are above
my understanding.'* (Rousseau, 1762)

The vicar then moves on to explain man's place in this ordered,
designed world. He raises the problem of evil. If God is good
and the universe so harmonious, why is there so much evil and
suffering? The vicar solves the problem of this paradox with an
appeal to free will. Humankind is free – our minds are not bound
by the laws of physics. Rousseau here asserts a type of dualism,
whereby the body is physical but the mind immaterial. While
the material body is dependent on the laws of nature (that is, the
laws that rule material bodies; the biological mechanism of our
bodies), the mind is not made of matter and therefore does not
abide by the law of nature. It doesn't change, die or decay, as bodies
do. Animals must follow their instincts and cannot do otherwise
(they cannot reflect on their actions or choices or tell themselves
they could have chosen differently), but humans have a free mind
which allows them to rise above their bodily instincts.

The vicar goes on to explain the consequence of this: if God made
us free to choose between good and evil, then it is humankind, not
God, that is the source of evil. No other animal is 'evil', as they do
not have access to self-reflection or conscious free choice. While
conscience and our innate feeling of compassion and pity can act
as a guide, it does not mean that humans are only capable of good.
If this were true, we would not have free will (because 'good' can't
be a choice if it is the only option). Moral virtue is innate in us but
we have to choose to follow it. To be moral is an act of the will.
The vicar goes on to explain that a person 'chooses between good

and evil as he judges between truth and falsehood; if his judgment is at fault, he chooses amiss', therefore choosing an act of evil does not make the person evil. It is not natural for a man who steals or who kills to feel content or happy; human nature dictates that he feel remorse and sadness.

Controversially Democratic Religion

In itself, Rousseau's view of God isn't too controversial. He said that we cannot know the essence of God, but God makes himself known to us through religious experience and the forces of nature. A benevolent God allows the existence of evil so that man can be free. To be moral, Rousseau argues, is to follow one's conscience, which is natural and God-given.

What did make this section controversial was the idea that such truths about God, humankind and our place in the world can be discovered by anyone, just by listening to one's heart. This idea effectively makes organized religion redundant, and so such an idea is antithetical to the Church and everything it preaches. In *Émile*, the vicar advocates natural religion with no rituals, no priest, and no Church. It is a religion whereby one fulfils one's own moral duties, where prayer is private and is a means to communicate on a personal level with God, the Supreme Being.

This attack on the Church, in such an open manner, was largely unprecedented in Rousseau's time and showed great courage and individuality. While it left Rousseau open to many attacks and made him deeply unpopular with the Church, the book *Émile* itself has been credited with influencing the way the educated classes raised their children, as well as serving as a paradigm for subsequent educational philosophers.

Conclusion

In this book we considered various aspects of Rousseau's philosophy: human nature, political thought, moral philosophy and education. However, all these theories and arguments are tightly knit in a clear system of thought where certain key ideas dominate. First, that states and societies are corrupt, and second, that we must find a way to overcome that corruption. Rousseau believed that inequality comes into being through societies and states, and that in a natural 'uncivilized' state, humans are free. He argued that with our capacity for free will, we have the potential to be virtuous – to choose good over evil – but everywhere we look people have become selfish, self-interested, debased and alienated. Rousseau sees this corruption of humankind as an evil – a moral evil – which needs to be put right. This can be done first in the private sphere, with an education for children which focuses first on developing their senses, and then on fostering reason and judgment, which are necessary for them to become moral beings. This education should take place in a just state where citizens are able to express their moral and political freedom as part of a General Will.

Rousseau was truly a revolutionary thinker, attending to the thinking of the time but also at odds with it. While much of his thought was influenced by natural law thinkers, philosophers of the Enlightenment and empiricism, he rejected the domination of reason, atheism and materialism. It is a healthy, non-envious love for oneself, for others and for God, he said, that allows individuals to flourish and society to progress.

Rousseau's influence on political and philosophical movements cannot be underestimated. One of the founding fathers of the United States, Thomas Jefferson (1743–1826), famously argued that 'all men are created equal but they are endowed by their creator with certain unalienable rights,' which echoed these lines from *The Social Contract*, written just 15 years earlier: 'the people are the sovereign in every state, and […] their rights are inalienable'. A republican thinker, Rousseau argued that a good state is not one where the majority rules, but where the General Will, as a unified whole, rules. He argued for freedom, but not negative freedom or freedom from constraints; instead he wanted to see a freedom focused on the people's right to rule and to determine their own destiny as members of a state. A good state, for Rousseau, is one ruled by the people for the people.

Rousseau has often been criticized as either a utopian (on the basis that people cannot relinquish their self interest in political matters) or an advocate of totalitarianism (because some of the most brutal leaders of the French revolution such as Maximilien de Robespierre saw him as their greatest inspiration). While this has blackened Rousseau's name, he never advocated violence and his famous claim that in obeying the General Will, people 'should be forced to be free' was never intended to support the most oppressive of regimes. Instead Rousseau's intention was to save humans from a tyranny and enslavement that they themselves were unaware of. They must therefore be saved from themselves; they must be forced to realize that they could be free by creating a just state where they themselves make the laws.

One important idea that we can take from Rousseau's philosophy is his critique of representative democracy, which for him is incompatible with republican principles. When electing representatives, people are free only when they vote; they then relinquish their freedom to representatives. Representative democracy can only work in large states if the representatives elected are held accountable for their decisions and follow the interests of the people they represent.

Leo Damrosch, in his biography of Rousseau, calls him a 'restless genius', and it's true that Rousseau had a difficult life, spending many years in exile. He never felt accepted in Geneva – his place of birth – nor in France or Italy. He was a difficult man to get along with by all accounts, which resulted in all his relationships being problematic. His thinking was often at odds with his peers, and his courage to stand by and vocalize his beliefs made him deeply unpopular. While there are many who disagree with Rousseau's ideas, it cannot be denied that he was one of the greatest philosophers of all time. His ability to overcome prejudice and assumptions, his desire to question established values and systems, and his indomitable spirit and love for humanity are what set him apart and ensure his place in history.

Bibliography

Barker Ernest (1946) *Social Contract: Essays by Locke, Hume and Rousseau.* Oxford University Press.

Berlin, I. (1969) 'Two Concepts of Liberty' in I. Berlin, *Four Essays on Liberty.* London: Oxford University Press. New Ed. in Berlin 2002.

Cohen Joshua (2010) *Rousseau: A Free Community of Equals.* Oxford University Press.

Cottret, Monique and Bernard Cottret (2011) *Jean-Jacques Rousseau en son temps.* Librairie Académique, Perrin, France.

Dent, Nicholas (2005) *Rousseau.* Routledge.

Glazier, J. (1982) 'Shakespeare, Montaigne, and the Idea of Savagery'. *Central Issues in Anthropology.* 4: 1-16. doi:10.1525/cia.1982.4.2.1.

Hodgen, M. (1964) *Early Anthropology in the sixteenth and seventeenth centuries.* Philadelphia: University of Pennsylvania Press.

Kennedy, Rosanne Terese (2012) *Rousseau in Drag.* Palgrave Macmillan.

Nisbet, Robert A. (1943) 'Rousseau and Totalitarianism'. *The Journal of Politics.* Vol. 5, No. 2 (May, 1943), pp. 93–114.

Parel, Anthony and Thomas Flanagan, eds. (1979) *Theories of Property, Aristotle to the Present.* Wilfred Laurier University Press.

Rosenblatt, Helena (1997) *Rousseau and Geneva: From the First Discourse to The Social Contract, 1749–1762.* Press Syndicate of the University of Cambridge.

Rosenblatt, Helena (2006) 'Rousseau's Gift to Geneva'. *CUNY Academic Works.* Available at: http://academicworks.cuny.edu/gc_pubs/223 Accessed March 2020.

Rousseau, Jean-Jacques (1782) *The Confessions.* Oxford University Press (This edition 2008).

Rousseau, Jean-Jacques (1754) *A Discourse on Inequality.* Penguin (This edition 2003).

Rousseau, Jean-Jacques (1762) *Émile.* Everyman Paperbacks (This edition 1993).

Saastamoinen, Kari (2010) 'Pufendorf on Natural Equality, Human Dignity, and Self Esteem'. *Journal of the History of Ideas.* Vol. 71, No. 1, (Jan. 2010), pp. 39–62. Available at: www.jstor.org/stable/20621922. Accessed 14 Mar 2020.

Spector, Céline (2019) *Rousseau.* Cambridge: Polity Press.

Weiss, Penny (1993) *Gendered Community: Rousseau, Sex and Politics.* NYU Press.

Whatmore, Richard (2012) *Against War and Empire: Geneva, Britain and France in the Eighteenth Century.* Yale University Press.

Wokler, Robert (2001) *Rousseau: A Very Short Introduction.* Oxford University Press.

Biography

Originally from France, Cressida gained her degree in French literature from the Université de Bretagne Occidentale in 2000 before completing a Masters degree in French literature and culture at King's College London in 2002. She has been a teacher in philosophy at a leading sixth form college in North London for 16 years, and has written college material and student guides for Philosophy and Religious Studies A level for Hodder Education. Cressida lives in Middlesex, England.

Acknowledgements

Special thanks for Alice at Bowden & Brazil, for giving me this opportunity and for all her work editing this book. I would also like to thank my family for their patience and support during the writing process and my colleagues and students at Woodhouse College for their encouragement and good humour.

Dedication

To Dad.

Picture Credits

Fig. 1 '"Les Charmettes" where Rousseau stayed with Mme de Warens'. Jacmin (https://commons.wikimedia.org/wiki/File:Les_Charmettes. jpg), "Les Charmettes", https://creativecommons.org/licenses/by-sa/3.0/ legalcode. **Fig. 2** 'Diderot's Encyclopedia'. (https://commons.wikimedia.org/ wiki/File:Encyclopedie_de_D'Alembert_et_Diderot_-_Premiere_Page_-_ ENC_1-NA5.jpg), "Encyclopedie de D'Alembert et Diderot - Premiere Page - ENC 1-NA5", marked as public domain, more details on Wikimedia Commons: https://commons.wikimedia.org/wiki/Template:PD-old. **Fig. 3** 'Portrait of Jean-Jacques Rousseau painted by Maurice Quentin de La Tour in 1753'. Maurice Quentin de La Tour creator QS:P170,Q314655 (https:// commons.wikimedia.org/wiki/File:Jean-Jacques_Rousseau_(painted_ portrait).jpg), "Jean-Jacques Rousseau (painted portrait)", marked as public domain, more details on Wikimedia Commons: https://commons.wikimedia. org/wiki/Template:PD-old. **Fig. 4** 'The tomb of Jean-Jacques Rousseau in the Panthéon in Paris, France'. Marko Kudjerski from Toronto, Canada (https:// commons.wikimedia.org/wiki/File:Tomb_of_Jean-Jacques_Rousseau_1,_ Paris_29_September_2012.jpg), "Tomb of Jean-Jacques Rousseau 1, Paris 29 September 2012", https://creativecommons.org/licenses/by/2.0/legalcode. **Fig. 5** 'Denis Diderot painted by Louis-Michel van Loo in 1767'. Louis-Michel van Loo creator QS:P170,Q381299 Unknown author (https:// commons.wikimedia.org/wiki/File:Denis_Diderot_111.PNG), "Denis Diderot 111", marked as public domain, more details on Wikimedia Commons: https://commons.wikimedia.org/wiki/Template:PD-old. **Fig. 6** 'Émile and the Savoyard Vicar in an etching created in 1777 for Émile by Jean-Michel Moreau (1741–1814)'. Jean-Michel Moreau (https://commons. wikimedia.org/wiki/File:Emile_et_le_vicaire_savoyard.jpg), "Emile et le vicaire savoyard", marked as public domain, more details on Wikimedia Commons: https://commons.wikimedia.org/wiki/Template:PD-old.

Other titles in this series:

Who the hell is?

This exciting new series of books sets out to explore the life and theories of the world's leading intellectuals in a clear and understandable way. The series currently includes the following subject areas:

Art History
Psychology
Philosophy
Sociology
Politics

For more information about forthcoming titles in the Who the Hell is...? series, go to **www.whothehellis.co.uk**

If any of our readers would like to put in a request for a particular intellectual to be included in our series, then please contact us at **info@whothehellis.co.uk**